How Successful Engineers Become Great Business Leaders

How Successful Engineers Become Great Business Leaders

Paul Rulkens

How Successful Engineers Become Great Business Leaders
Copyright © Business Expert Press, LLC, 2018.

All rights reserved. No part of this publication may be reproduced, stored in a retrieval system, or transmitted in any form or by any means—electronic, mechanical, photocopy, recording, or any other except for brief quotations, not to exceed 250 words, without the prior permission of the publisher.

First published in 2018 by
Business Expert Press, LLC
222 East 46th Street, New York, NY 10017
www.businessexpertpress.com

ISBN-13: 978-1-94784-368-4 (paperback)
ISBN-13: 978-1-94784-369-1 (e-book)

Business Expert Press Human Resource Management and Organizational Behavior Collection

Collection ISSN: 1946-5637 (print)
Collection ISSN: 1946-5645 (electronic)

Illustrations: Studio Dona
Photo author: Marc Schols

Cover and interior design by S4Carlisle Publishing Services Private Ltd., Chennai, India

First edition: 2018

10 9 8 7 6 5 4 3 2 1

Printed in the United States of America.

Abstract

High performance expert Paul Rulkens provides the inside advice you need to accelerate your career as a business leader with an engineering background—from building on your unique strengths to achieving big business goals.

How Successful Engineers Become Great Business Leaders is full of thought-provoking insights, practical applications, and pragmatic techniques to help you get everything you can out of everything you have. You don't have to be ill in order to get better. Whether you're an experienced business executive, corporate manager, or ambitious professional, this book will show you how to apply your specific engineering strengths to:

- Maximize your skill and talent to accelerate your career
- Grow your business with the least amount of effort
- Set and achieve ambitious business goals
- Focus on strategic quitting to raise the performance bar
- Avoid behaviors that mask your strengths
- Create a high-performance execution culture
- Improve your own executive judgment
- Build long-term client relationships
- Develop a blueprint to become an unstoppable goal achiever

The road to business success for leaders with engineering backgrounds is common and predictable, but not always obvious: There is a method to the madness. This unique book will show you how.

Keywords

business leadership, engineers, goals, high-performance organization, career, business growth, strategy execution

Contents

Foreword ix
Acknowledgments xi
Introduction xiii

Part I	How the Best Get Better 1	
Chapter 1	Big Business Goals 3	
Part II	Do You Have a Vision, or Are You Just Seeing Things? 17	
Chapter 2	Perfect Clarity 19	
Part III	Even Michael Jordan Plays a Lousy Basketball Game in the Dark 31	
Chapter 3	Engineering Strengths 33	
Chapter 4	Overcoming Obstacles 53	
Chapter 5	Effective Leadership Behaviors 69	
Part IV	If You Think You're in Control, You're Not Going Fast Enough 85	
Chapter 6	Strategic Quitting 87	
Chapter 7	Improving Executive Judgment 101	
Chapter 8	Eliminating Adverse Habits 115	
Chapter 9	Building Client Connections 127	
Part V	The Unstoppable Goal Achiever 137	
Chapter 10	Goal-Achieving Blueprint 139	

Summary of How Engineers Become Business Leaders 149
30 Executive Questions to Improve Your Business Leadership 151
Summary of the Goal-Achieving Blueprint 155
Recommended Reading 157
About the Author 159
Index 161

Foreword

How does an engineer become a business leader? If I take myself as an example, my career path gave me a fascinating and broad experience. I have spent the first 10 years of my career in different manufacturing roles. This gave me the opportunity to apply my engineering training on a deep level. After that, I was offered an HR management development role at headquarters. It gave me a close insight in the roles and responsibilities of many other disciplines, such as marketing and sales and R&D. This really opened my world. My perspective was further expanded when I moved from Europe to Brazil and assumed full responsibility of the company's country operation. As a leader, I was suddenly involved in maintaining key contacts with governments, legal affairs, clients, etc. My work as a corporate executive has covered broad areas, such as risk-based auditing, safety, and leadership of worldwide operations. As the managing director of the NAP and DACE foundation, my current responsibility is to enhance the knowledge and network within the Dutch process industry chain in general on one side and the development of the profession of cost and value engineers on the other.

This brings me to a subject that is close to my heart: How can engineers accelerate their business careers? This is especially important, since the business field has changed for engineers. We operate within many more boundaries, for example, those set by standard work-processes, corporate rules, and law. Furthermore, business focus has shifted to shorter term results. This means less freedom for engineers who want to develop themselves. At the same time, individual engineers need to take much more personal responsibility for their career path and growth to business leadership. This requires a different mindset. Due to this changed environment, coaching by senior management is under pressure as well. And we can help them with that.

In the past, the path to career advancement was simply to become a more effective engineer, after which you get the opportunity to broaden your skills and experience. Nowadays, it's no longer enough to climb the engineering ladder, but you need to become aware of which business ladder you are actually climbing. An engineering education, focused on the details of how to become a successful engineer, will not prepare you for this shift in thinking. Control is an essential part of the engineering training, yet the ambitious engineer needs to let go of control and step into the unknown to achieve business success. This requires climbing different ladders, trying different things with the confidence that your engineering skills and abilities will support you to be successful in other parts of a business as well.

I have known Paul Rulkens from my days as a senior operations executive with DSM. The first time we met, he helped my global manufacturing leadership team to set a new vision and especially think out of the box. It's therefore no surprise to me that he has written this book for leaders with an engineering background who want to continue to do things differently to accelerate their career. We share a common philosophy around leadership for engineers and that's why we founded Quantum Leap: a master program to accelerate the careers of high potential leaders with an engineering background.

How successful engineers become great business leaders provides a pragmatic approach to find a balance between optimizing your job and preparing for the next step in business leadership. This is recommended reading, not only for every leader with an engineering background who wants to boost his or her career, but also for senior managers that support these leaders as well.

Jan-Willem Sanders
cofounder Quantum Leap Master Program

Acknowledgments

My gratitude to Francesca Gambardella, Anneriëtte Rulkens, Riet Rulkens, Wim Rulkens, and Heidi Pozzo for their valuable comments and insights.

Thank you Alan Weiss for inspiring me to always think bigger.

I am very thankful to Jan-Willem Sanders: We share the same passion and excitement to help business leaders with an engineering background.

Thank you Paresh Bhakta, Marcel Berkhout, Stépan Breedveld, Jian, Aloys Krechting, Erik Oostwegel, Guus Pelzer, and Luca Rosetto for sharing your perspectives with me.

Deep appreciation goes to the wonderful BEP team: Charlene Kronstedt and Rob Zwettler.

My thanks to my editor Dorseda de Block, my graphic designer Marieke Dona, and my digital strategist Jan Scheele.

Introduction

Why This Book

The brilliant yet borderline insane poet William Blake once wrote, "Eternity is in love with the productions of time." I have always felt that the ability to design, create, and produce useful things that have enhanced the happiness of billions of people, now and far into the future, is a noble calling. It's the calling of an engineer. Interestingly enough, this calling often extends to engineers taking up the mantle of leadership as well. Since more than 30 percent of Fortune 500 CEOs have a degree in engineering, the field is clearly a stepping stone to business leadership at the highest level.

Engineers traditionally grow into leaders, either by exposure to valuable experience outside the engineering profession or through additional training to broaden one's perspective, such as an MBA.

Gaining valuable experience is a slow process. It can take decades before talented and ambitious engineers rise to the top, especially since classic engineering jobs typically require in-depth mastery of niche subjects. Thus, it may take a long time and a lot of patience before an engineer has the opportunity to broaden his or her experience. In our rapidly changing world, since patience is in short supply, this career pathway will undoubtedly become less attractive in the future.

A typical MBA education, on the other hand, may carry significant downsides as well. Many MBAs apply a kind of cookie-cutter approach to help students grow quickly into business leaders. The assumption is that educational approaches and business insights that work for lawyers, accountants, and sales people will work for professionals with an engineering background as well. It often ignores the fact that leveraging specific strengths of those with an engineering background may be the fastest and most viable pathway to leadership success.

I therefore propose a third approach: By understanding and leveraging the strengths of leaders with engineering experience to achieve ambitious business goals, we may open a faster, smoother, and more enjoyable track to leadership success.

This concept brings me to the main question of this book: *How can business leaders with an engineering past apply their strengths to accelerate their leadership career trajectories?*

Who Will Benefit Most from This Book

In the past 20 years, my career has covered three stages. I started as a chemical engineer, designing, building, and running big chemical plants all over the world. I then moved into business leadership, with a focus on strategy, innovation, and building a high-performance organization. Currently, as a high-performance leadership expert and a trusted boardroom advisor, I'm in stage three. The insights I share with you in this book are therefore based on personal, practical observations of leadership behaviors and personal, pragmatic application of leadership ideas. I have codified my experience and distilled the most useful and actionable ideas for leadership success.

This book is written for three groups of people. The first group comprises the senior business executives, who are not only looking for ways to improve their own personal performance, but especially the performance of managers with an engineering background in their teams. This book helps develop these managers to gain a broad perspective, look at business through the lens of their bosses and think like senior business leaders. The second group are the managers with an engineering background, looking for ways to rapidly accelerate their business careers. This book provides a practical strategy to quickly create additional business value, which helps set them apart from the competition. The third group are the professionals with engineering backgrounds. The ideas from this book will be useful to develop and show advanced leadership skills and behaviors in their existing jobs to rapidly improve performance.

How This Book Is Organized

Marcus Aurelius, the Roman philosopher and Emperor, observed that the secret of winning lies in the organization of the nonobvious. This book could have been written as a general essay on leadership and goal-achieving. My objective, however, was different. I wanted to find and organize the nonobvious that would be especially relevant for leaders who were former engineers. This endeavor led me to choose a common thread for this book: *How can leaders with an engineering background organize their specific skills and unique talents to reach big goals in a nonobvious way?*

To answer this question, the book is organized into five parts:

Part I: How the Best Get Better. This section puts business leadership success in perspective. Chapter 1, *Big Business Goals*, answers the question: How can you maximize your odds of great leadership success in business? Here I will make the case that goal-achieving should be the core mindset of any business leader, including those with an engineering background. I will also argue that the best business leaders get better by a relentless focus on growth goals. Furthermore, it introduces the three building blocks of goal achieving: clarity, focus, and execution.

Part II: Do You Have a Vision, or Are You Just Seeing Things? The second part of the book explores the first building block of goal achieving: clarity. Chapter 2, *Perfect Clarity*, addresses how a leadership vision can be turned into tangible business goals. It provides a practical approach to how leaders can clarify their most important business growth objectives and make the right connections to make those objectives happen.

Part III: Even Michael Jordan Plays a Lousy Basketball Game in the Dark. The next part of the book is about the second building block of goal achieving: focus. It describes three elements to maintain focus on your goals.

- Chapter 3, *Engineering Strengths*, explains how engineers can build on their three main strengths—reality-based thinking, process design, and accelerated learning.
- Chapter 4, *Overcoming Obstacles*, introduces several strategies to use these main strengths to deal with setbacks on the bumpy road toward accomplishing big goals.
- Chapter 5, *Effective Leadership Behaviors*, explains how any leader can use behavioral distinctions to create language, metaphors, and stories to maintain focus on building a company culture that makes achieving big goals possible.

Part IV: If You Think You're in Control, You're Not Going Fast Enough. The fourth part deals with the last building block of goal achieving: execution: How can leaders maintain momentum and continue to move toward their most important goals? This part of the book contains four elements.

- Chapter 6, *Strategic Quitting*, explains how your ability to strategically quit initiatives equals your ability to succeed. This chapter illustrates how engineers can use their unique strengths to stop unimportant activities. This provides the time, money, and energy to set and achieve new goals.
- Chapter 7, *Improving Executive Judgment*, deals with the behavioral pitfalls that may sabotage execution power, and how your unique talents as an engineer will help avoid costly mistakes.
- Chapter 8, *Eliminating Adverse Habits*, explains how a great leader is able to get rid of unhelpful habits, which actually mask strengths and impair goal-achieving abilities. You will find an in-depth discussion of the typical unhelpful habits that actually mask the strengths of leaders with an engineering background.
- Chapter 9, *Building Client Connections*, is based on the idea that nothing happens unless a sale is made: every executive has to bring in business. To achieve growth goals, the ability to grow a company by expanding the customer base is therefore essential. This chapter shows how to use engineering strengths to design a referral system that creates the relationships necessary to support business growth.

Part V: The Unstoppable Goal Achiever. The final part of this book brings the three building blocks of goal achieving—clarity, focus, and execution—and the three unique strengths of leaders with an engineering background—reality-based thinking, process design, and accelerated learning—together. Chapter 10, *Goal-Achieving Blueprint*, provides an actionable goal-achieving template to immediately get started with the ideas in this book.

Figure A shows the relationship between all five parts of the book.

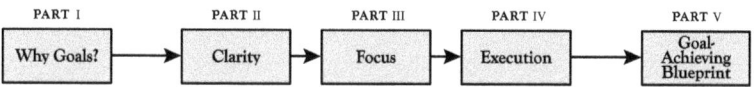

Figure A How this book is organized

How to Use This Book

When professionals, such as engineers, are moving to leadership roles, it's necessary to build additional skills and especially show different behaviors. At various places in this book, I have therefore highlighted actionable leadership skills with short paragraphs, titled *Practical Application*. Furthermore, by regularly asking how an idea from the book can be implemented by the reader, I have provided actionable leadership insights to show different behaviors. These implementation opportunities are titled *Executive Questions*. Finally, I have included several interviews with senior business leaders to provide an outside view on how successful engineers become great business leaders. These interviews are titled *External Perspective*.

Archilochus, the ancient Greek poet, observed that a fox knows many things, but a hedgehog knows one important thing. My hope is that after reading this book, you will act like a fox and think like hedgehog. The big thing is that there is a method to the madness of how successful engineers become great business leaders. It's up to you to act on the many ideas from this book to make it happen.

PART I
How the Best Get Better

CHAPTER 1

Big Business Goals

How can you maximize your odds of great leadership success in business?

Why Big Business Goals Matter

In the iconic movie *Pulp Fiction*, viewers are introduced to a character called Mr. Wolf. He shows up on the scene to clean up the sordid mess created by the two main characters of the movie. The mess includes a dead body, an upset wife, and a blood-covered car. In the entire scene, Mr. Wolf doesn't lift a finger but is very effective by simply telling others exactly what to do. He solves big problems with the least amount of energy. This, of course, is why I like his character so much.

To be an engineer is to solve problems and achieve goals. This is the raison d'être. This is why you do what you do. In secret, the actual fantasy of many engineers is to be Mr. or Ms. Wolf. When the Bat-sign lights up in the sky, you move in, solve the problem, briefly bask in the adoration of the crowd, and make a dramatic exit to deal with the next crisis. This heroic image solidifies our thinking that becoming better at problem solving will help us to become better leaders as well. After all, the reward for solving complex problems is the opportunity to solve even more complex problems. Yet what has got you here won't get you there. The differences between a successful engineer and a great business leader are better skills and behaviors to solve different problems and achieve different goals.

It's therefore a good moment to introduce an interesting question: How can you use your engineering backgrounds to solve bigger and bigger problems and rapidly become outstanding leaders? This may be the greatest hurdle you will face in your entire career. The corollary to this question is, of course: Why is it that some engineers become outstanding business leaders and achieve big business goals, while others, talented as they may be, never rise to the top? To answer this question, you may need a better understanding of the role of skill, luck, and talent.

Why Skill, Luck, and Talent Drive Achievement

About 5 years ago, a group of senior executives enthusiastically told me that the massive success of their business was driven by an excellent strategy and a culture of getting things done. They were right about the nature of their results. Rumor had it that a money-printing press was in full operation in the bowels of their factories. They were wrong, however, about the reason for their splendid results. Within 2 years, the business came to a grinding and unexpected halt. After a painful restructuring, the business has recently been sold, the workforce has been reduced, and profitability still seems a distant dream.

This tragic story is an illustration of the illusion of control. It happens when you assign too much credit for your success to your own skills and talent, while underestimating the significant role of luck.

The formula for achievement is both profound and simple:

$$\text{achievement} = \text{skill} + \text{talent} + \text{luck}$$

A skill is applied knowledge or ability that leads to a predictable and consistent way to achieve a predefined result. Usually, it requires a combination of experience and training. A skill is therefore learnable.

Talent, on the other hand, is driven by the natural inclination toward a skill and generally determines the ceiling of a skill. For example, someone who loves working with numbers will achieve more in mathematics than someone who doesn't, even if their experience, intelligence, and training in the field of mathematics are the same.

Luck is the happy circumstance in which our skills and talents may bloom. For example, the gains of a roulette player completely depend on luck. His skills and talents are limited to choosing a number or a color, moving a pile of chips, waiting for the feedback and then repeating the process. It's as simple as that. On the other hand, the achievement of a chess master is determined mostly by skill and talent. Yet even during a chess match, luck can still play a significant role: A spicy Thai meal from

Figure 1.1 *Intersection of skill, luck, and talent for extraordinary achievement*

the evening before may upset his stomach, and as a result deep thinking may be compromised by ungainly bowel movements at essential moments during the match.

To achieve success, you therefore have to operate at the intersection of skill, talent, and luck (see Figure 1.1).

If you are skilled and talented yet unlucky, you will forever be a best-kept secret. With skills and luck but lacking talent, you may make it to tier two, yet tier one will stay out of reach. With only talent and luck, you won't be able to maintain momentum and run the risk of becoming a one-day wonder. Only with skill, talent, and luck will you be able to achieve outstanding results.

The two variables you are able to control as a leader to achieve extraordinary results are the development of skill and the application of talent. Development requires awareness of the skill, a decision to develop it, and, finally, the hard part: consistent actions to improve the skill. The difficult part of talent application, however, is often simply becoming aware of your talents. You may be brilliant at free-diving, a form of underwater diving that relies on the ability to hold your breath until resurfacing: No use of a breathing apparatus such as an oxygen tank is allowed. If you have never tried free-diving, you may be completely unaware of having this talent. That's why it's called a hidden talent. The truth is there's much more you haven't tried than what you have tried. Thus, the majority of knowledge about your talents are actually hidden. That's also why the most important parts of your extensive library are the books you haven't read.

Why We Overestimate Skill and Talent

There are two reasons you habitually overestimate your skill and talent and underestimate the role of luck. The first is the *Dunning–Kruger effect*—a cognitive bias in which unskilled individuals suffer from illusory superiority, mistakenly rating their abilities much higher than average. This bias is attributed to a metacognitive inability of the unskilled to recognize their mistakes. It means that if you are completely ignorant and unskilled in a certain area, you may overestimate how well you will perform in this area. During a TV cooking program, the master chef made the task of cutting carrots look easy. Only when I heard that it requires a full year of advanced master chef training to learn how to properly cut vegetables did I realize there is much more to cutting vegetables than meets the eye. This is the Dunning–Kruger effect in action. Most people have no problem recognizing this effect in others. Think of surveys where more than 50 percent of vehicle operators consistently believe they are within the top 10 percent of safe drivers. You think you're skilled, but in reality you're simply lucky. As a general rule, if you encounter the Dunning–Kruger effect in others, keep in mind the words of Mark Twain: "Never argue with ignorant people. They will bring you down to their level and beat you with experience."

The second reason is *cargo cult thinking*. The term cargo cult was first coined after World War II. During the conflict, several remote-island-based airfields were established for military purposes, baffling the indigenous, primitive populations. Often limited or no contact was established between the islanders and the more modern military forces. When the military finally left the islands, the original inhabitants tried to recreate the airfields using bamboo, stone, and other available material, waiting for the planes to return. Hence the name cargo cult thinking: If you build it, they will come.

Cargo cult thinking is not limited to the minds of our primitive brothers and sisters. It has a prominent place in modern business thinking as well. We often believe that if we simply emulate the visible effects of achievement, the real achievement will follow automatically. Especially when the initial results look promising, we tend to think we are skilled, while in reality, we are lucky. For instance, Elizabeth Holmes, the notorious CEO of Theranos, started wearing a black turtleneck to mimic

Steve Jobs in order to practice a reality distortion of her own. Though initially very successful, as the recent scandals around Theranos have shown, what she actually did was mix cause and effect: The rooster that crows in the morning doesn't cause the sun to rise. Likewise, cajoling the rooster to crow earlier will not make a longer day.

The absence of skill and talent and underestimating the role of luck are dangerous follies and the main reasons smart people sometimes do stupid things. The fact that there are lottery winners is no excuse for buying lottery tickets. Instead, you need to move to a place where skill and talent massively trump reliance on luck. Fertile land beats better seeds all the time. In order to find fertile land, you need to turn to the *power laws*.

How to Use Power Laws

Nature is unbalanced, and therefore output isn't necessarily determined by the size of input. For example, in the English language, fewer than 3,000 words are used more than 80 percent of the time. This law is known as the 80/20 rule, Pareto rule, or vital few. Only small chunks matter, especially when it comes to achievement. Our focus is to find fertile lands, where talents and skill can be maximized and the influence of luck can be minimized. The reason to minimize the role of luck is that you want your achievements to be sustainable. The fertile lands are marked by power laws. A power law describes how small differences can yield exponential results. For our discussion, we need to focus on the power laws of prime location, prime time, and prime knowledge.

A great example of the *power law of prime location* happened on January 12, 2007, when the world-class violin player Joshua Bell played for an audience of over 1,000 people. Interestingly enough, he played while dressed as a common street artist in the subway of Washington D.C. Mostly ignored by the apathetic and rushed subway crowd, it took him almost 45 minutes to earn a meager 30 dollars. A few weeks later, Bell played again, but now in Carnegie Hall, which was packed to its limits with ecstatic listeners who loved his work. In both cases, his talents and skill were identical, yet the results were vastly different. What changed was the influence of luck. The crowd at Carnegie Hall was self-selecting, yet the chance that the subway crowd would recognize and value Bell's work was limited at best. By choosing a different venue, the reliance on luck to achieve success became much smaller.

Executive Question

Where is the prime area or location where your talents and skills will have maximum effect to improve your business?

The *power law of prime time* can be illustrated by understanding airplane pilot skills. The most important moments when flying an airplane are landing, taking off, and emergencies. An airplane pilot who crosses the Atlantic Ocean will spend less than 10 percent of his or her time doing these three activities. The remaining time will be spent on routine activities like watching the autopilot. A pilot who wants to step up the game and become better will need to focus on improving skills in landing, taking off, and emergencies. On January 15, 2009, US Airways pilot Chesley Sullenberger managed to make a successful emergency landing with his Airbus A-320 on the Hudson River. Pulling off this feat requires incredible skill, and, fortunately, Sullenberger had recently trained for peak performance during such a scenario, thus reducing the reliance on luck.

Executive Question

What are your prime chunks of time as a business leader, and how can you maximize their effect?

Finally, the *power law of prime knowledge* is especially applicable to knowledge workers. Bill Gates once remarked that a great lathe operator commands several times the wage of an average lathe operator, but a great writer of software code is worth 10,000 times the price of an average software writer. This means the impact of knowledge is often subject to power laws as well: By focusing on expanding the right skills, a great software writer doesn't need much luck to command a high salary.

Executive Question

Which additional knowledge would have an exponential impact on your achievement as a business leader?

Why Small Differences Create Extraordinary Achievements

Joshua Bell and, of course, Bill Gates are on top of their games. Their applications of the power laws result in a huge disparity in results and compensation between the absolute top performers and the muddling middle. First prize: a Ferrari. Second price: a set of steak knives. The power laws therefore open ways to real achievement. This phenomenon is called the razor's edge, and it means that small differences, consistently applied, will have a huge impact on your results. Part of these differences are driven by luck. If Bill Gates had caught the flu the day he and the owners of an obscure software company called Seattle Computer Products were hammering out a deal, IBM would not have adopted MS-DOS as the operating standard for all its hardware and the company Microsoft as you know it now would probably not have existed.

Another part of these small differences is driven by talent and skill. The excellent software code writer who is paid 10 times more than the average code writer obviously doesn't have 10 times more skill and talent, but is only slightly better in the areas that truly matter.

Here lies the heart of extraordinary achievement. If you want to double your results, you don't have to double your skills, but you need to apply the power laws to become slightly better at what truly matters.

How the Link between Risk and Reward Drives Achievement

Next to the power laws, there's another law that will help you become great business leaders and achieve massive success. This is the *law of risk and reward*. This law tells us the reward you get is equal to the risk you are willing to take. Take, for example, long-term stock market investment strategies. The big secret of the investment world is that your exposure to risk determines your maximum reward. Penny stocks, for instance, provide the highest possible returns but will expose you to dramatic losses as well, as penny stocks can lose all their value overnight. If you invest in less risky assets such as government bonds, your rewards will be significantly lower. Therefore, a typical successful investment strategy is based on a portfolio consisting of relatively secure bonds and relatively risky equities.

The same can be said of your business success. The more you expose yourself to risk, the higher the results can be. The problem, however, is that a massive downfall is more likely as well. For example, if you would apply the power law of knowledge to narrowly specialize and decide to become the best reservoir engineer in the world, you may find yourself in a comfortable winner-takes-all position. This position poses two problems. First of all, it takes a long time to become the best. Because of technological and societal developments, your deep expertise may also be irrelevant for future success. For example, your ability to solve complicated differential equations may have been much more valuable before the arrival of the computer. The second problem of narrow specialization is that the biggest rewards are usually not harvested by the originators of knowledge but by the people who apply this knowledge to improve the condition of a large number of people. This explains why Bill Gates is a billionaire many times over, while the top programmers at Microsoft do well but will never approach this level of financial success.

This means that if business leaders want to be successful, they need to expose themselves to more risky activities to gain the maximum rewards, while at the same time minimizing the downside of this risk exposure.

How Focus on Goals Maximizes Results

So far we have seen that the power laws of location, time, and knowledge may help to minimize the impact of luck and maximize the impact of skill and talent. Furthermore, we have discussed that the size of a reward equals the risk you are willing to take. Can the two be combined to present an actionable guideline to answer an important question: How to maximize achievement as a business leader with an engineering background?

One approach is descriptive. First, analyze the actions and careers of the most successful companies, organizations, and leaders. After that, distill the key skills and personality traits. Finally, present these skills and traits in an actionable menu to be used by anyone who wants to emulate success. The problem with this approach is twofold.

First, you may suffer from the *narrative fallacy*. By presenting a direct line between two points, you forget the role of luck and chance in the entire process. If Alexander Fleming had diligently cleaned all samples in his lab, he never would have made the chance discovery of antibiotics in one of his dirty petri dishes. This is why Jim Collins' book *Built to Last*, in which he used a narrative to describe the common traits of the most successful companies, didn't stand the test of time. After 15 years, a large number of his excellent companies have joined the ranks of mediocrity, or even failed completely.

Second, you may ignore the *Einstein observation*. One day, when Einstein was teaching physics at Oxford, he gave an exam to his senior class of physics students. After the exam, a baffled assistant asked why he had given the same exam to the same students 1 year ago. Einstein remarked dryly that the questions may have been the same but the answers had changed. The skills and talents leading to current success may no longer be applicable for a successful future.

I therefore prefer a more comprehensive and pragmatic approach to maximize achievement: Make business goals the core of your leadership focus.

How to Select the Right Goals

Life is about goals; all else is just commentary. If it weren't for goals, mankind's major achievements would have been the result of stumbling upon success by random, undirected activities. That doesn't mean it's impossible to combine success and random activities. After all, a million chimpanzees with a million typewriters may come up with Shakespeare's Hamlet after a million years. Many achievements are based on chance discoveries and lucky breaks. Yet the efforts were almost always driven by goal-oriented individuals. Ray McIntire invented Styrofoam purely by accident around the time of World War II while trying to achieve another goal: finding a flexible electrical insulator.

Goal achieving is about solving problems. You can apply problem-solving skills to return to a previous state or to move to a new and better state. The bigger your goals, the bigger the obstacles and the bigger the problems you will have to solve. An objective that doesn't require you to face obstacles is not a goal but an activity. Where is the fun in that?

If goal achieving becomes the core of your activities as a business leader, it's essential to pick the right goals and engage with the right activities. This means that your goal must be worthy of your attention. It needs to solve a pressing problem. Engineers usually have different problems than do senior business leaders. The engineer may have to deal with a new bridge, a nuclear reactor design, or implementation of a just-in-time delivery process. The business leader, on the other hand, must focus on *business development*. This means that goals need to improve the condition of the customer. While a better mousetrap may work, an innovative company expansion strategy with advanced robotics for widespread critter control is much better for business leadership success.

Practical Application

Here are six questions for a business leader to find out whether a new business goal should be considered:

- What exactly is the goal?
- Does the goal achieve a significant result?
- What are the options to achieve the goal?
- Are the options feasible to achieve the goal?
- Are the options effective to achieve the goal?
- Do the advantages of the options outweigh their disadvantages?

Furthermore, your business development goal must be connected to your existing talents and preferably linked to skills that you already possess or that can be developed easily. If a young Thomas Edison had decided to become an investment banker, the world would probably have gained a mediocre financial brain but would still be lit by candles.

To ensure sustainable achievement, your business development goal must cover an area where the role of luck is minimized. It's impossible to predict the future, yet several warning signs will tell you that luck may play too big a role:

- An existing field with winner-takes-all characteristics. It may not be a good use of your talents to try to beat the company Amazon at its own game. Instead, it's better to pick an underserved niche without existing dominant players.

- The need for long-term skill building. The training of a brain surgeon may take 10 years or more. The good news is there are few people who are willing to sacrifice this amount of time to gain the deep knowledge required to be successful. Thus, there are a limited number of brain surgeons commanding high salaries. The bad news is that many things can happen in 10 years' time. A brain surgeon robot may make the regular brain surgeon obsolete overnight.
- A singular, nontransferable skill niche. Business leadership skills can be broadly applied. Typewriter repair skills? Not so much.

Your business development goal must be susceptible to power laws in order to get extraordinary results in the quickest way possible. Small differences need to have extraordinary effects. This is why operating in a niche often has the biggest benefits. For example, in-depth advanced robotics knowledge may very well create a big chasm between you and your nearest competitor.

The risks associated with your business development goals must be as small as possible, while the rewards must be big. If a risk is big, it's important to find ways to mitigate the downside of risk before even trying to achieve your goals.

Practical Application

There are three ways to mitigate the downside of risk:

- *Transfer* risk to someone else, which is the core idea behind insurance.
- *Reduce* risk by setting big goals and, at the same time, committing to small investments of time, energy, and money at every step on your way to achieve the big goals.
- *Eliminate* risk. For example, while developing deep sea drilling, the risk of losing human life can be completely eliminated by using robots.

Which of these three strategies would be most applicable to reduce the risk profile of your biggest business goal?

Finally, your most important goals as a business leader must be focused on business growth. This change in focus separates the engineer from the business leader. Growth is the natural state of any organization or organism. If it stops growing, it withers and dies. Or, viewing this from another angle, if your business adds massive value to your customers, it would be unfortunate to stifle your own growth and deny this value to existing and new customers. The drive to achieve growth goals is therefore a key distinction for every successful business leader.

Summary and What's Next

Business success is a function of skill, talent, and luck. You can fully control your skill building and actively work on recognizing your talents. The power laws give you the opportunity to maximize the impact of your skills and talents, and minimize the role of luck. Small differences have an enormous impact on the final results. At the same time, you need to minimize your exposure to the downside of risk. The practical application of these insights is that goal achieving in the area of business growth should be the central focus of business leaders

Connecting to your skills and talents, minimizing the role of luck, adhering to the power laws, minimizing the downside of risk, and focusing on business growth will help you achieve the right goals. This is how your chances of business success can be maximized and how the best leaders get even better.

Now that we have discussed the importance of selecting business goals worthy of your time, we can now address the question: How can leaders with engineering backgrounds actually become outstanding goal achievers? Doing so requires answering three questions:

1. *What does success of big growth goals look like?* Succeeding with big goals requires clarity. Clarity is therefore the first building block of becoming an unstoppable achiever. Getting clarity as a business leader will be the focus of Part II of this book.
2. *How can you achieve big growth goals in the easiest, fastest, and most elegant way possible?* There are thousands of ways to achieve a goal. As a business leader with an engineering background, you will therefore

need to choose the few that truly build on your unique skills and talents. Choosing them requires focus: the second building block of becoming an unstoppable goal achiever. Focus is therefore the subject of Part III of the book.

3. *How can you consistently take action to make progress on big growth goals?* Once clarity and focus have been achieved, it's time to make your goals happen, which requires the ability to execute. Execution is therefore the third building block of becoming an outstanding goal achiever. Building execution power is the subject of Part IV of the book.

Finally, Part V of this book brings these elements together in an actionable blueprint for business leaders with an engineering background to make big growth goals happen.

PART II

Do You Have a Vision, or Are You Just Seeing Things?

CHAPTER 2

Perfect Clarity

How do you create perfect clarity about your goals as a business leader with an engineering background?

Why Perfect Clarity Matters

There are only two problems in your life, your business, and your career:

- What do you want?
- How do you get it?

These two questions are the core of goal achieving. This chapter deals with the first question and addresses where you want to go as a business leader with an engineering background. For this, you require not only clarity for yourself, but also the ability to describe this clarity to other people. This ability is needed because no single big goal has ever been achieved in isolation. For example, Albert Einstein was relatively weak in mathematics. He was keenly aware of this fact. While he developed the theory of relativity, he surrounded himself with a sophisticated team of skilled mathematicians to make sure all the mathematical details would work. The conclusion? Even the greatest minds will fail, if not actively supported by other people.

The twin engines of leadership for goal achieving are vision and connection. A vision describes where you want to go as a leader. Since every big goal requires help from other people, a connection ensures that others support you on the journey to achieve the goal. Figure 2.1 shows why both a vision and a connection are necessary for business leadership.

If both vision and connection are lacking, you are *stuck*. Leaders who are trapped in this quadrant typically find themselves paralyzed, reacting

	− CONNECTION +	
VISION +	Ivory Tower	High Performance
VISION −	Stuck	Campfire Songs

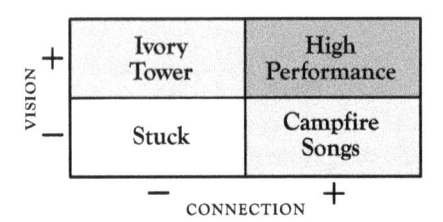

Figure 2.1 Vision and connection: The twin engines of leadership

to the world around them instead of trying to shape the world together with others. They have no idea where they are going, which coincidentally does not really matter, because they are traveling alone anyway.

If the vision is defined but the connection is missing, you end up in the *ivory tower*. This situation is characterized by conceptual thinking, detailed plans, and big ambitions. Yet, it lacks support to get things done. Typically, these leaders have developed many strategic plans, but all are now catching (cyber)dust in deep drawers or electronic files. Often, organizations develop peak activity at the start of defining a new strategy. After this peak, the fire to achieve strategic goals quickly burns out, things go back to normal and the usual routines are reinstated. It's a well-known pattern for big, complex projects driven by government subsidies. As soon as the written plans are accepted and all parties involved have received their money, many of these projects tend to die a slow and silent death.

Leaders who make excellent connections but lack vision operate in a *campfire songs* organization. This mindset usually becomes apparent at the typical corporate retreat. The management team metaphorically holds hands, sings campfire songs and puts team-building prominently on the map. Since vision is lacking, as soon as the team is back in the office, they continue the friendly camaraderie, but lack any movement toward a meaningful goal. This pattern is often encountered in organizations where the main focus is on pleasing, instead of serving. If you don't want to rock the boat, you will remain in the harbor. A boat is safest inside a harbor, but that's not what it's designed for.

Only when leaders both have a vision and are able to make a connection with others are they able to achieve extraordinary, high-performance results. How do you quickly build a vision and make a connection?

Why Mindsets Are Important to Achieve Goals

In 1998, after several ignominious defeats, the UK Olympic rowing team resolved to change its ways. In preparation for the big event, they agreed to ask themselves one question before making any decision: *Will it make the boat go faster?* For example, a party tonight? No, it will not make the boat go faster. An additional training tomorrow at 5 a.m.? Yes, it will. This simple, yet consistent approach to decision making provided a breakthrough. They won the Olympics 18 months later.

This success story is an example of a fascinating concept called the *psychology of achievement*. It tells us that *thoughts* lead to *feelings*, which lead to *actions* and finally *results*. Figure 2.2 illustrates this sequence.

Here's what happened to the UK rowing team. With a simple decision of adopting a different mindset with different thoughts regarding decision making, it was possible to take different actions and get very different results. This is how you win Olympic gold. This is also how you eat pizza. Dinner time (thoughts) leads to hunger (feeling), which leads to actions (order pizza), and finally results (eat). The psychology of achievement shows that your mindsets drive results.

Since achieving excellent results is all about mindsets and seems so simple, an interesting question would be *why is achieving great success still so enormously rare?* After all, if you feed your mind with high-performance thoughts, you generate high-performance feelings, take high-performance actions and, naturally, get high-performance results. Alas, things may not be that easy. Often your thinking is compromised. The first reason is *thinking in reverse*, where you take the existing results as a basis for future thinking. For example, a company has grown market share in the past 5 years, and predicts its future market share by simple extrapolation. In other words, you use your rear view mirror to predict what is ahead. This, of course, goes well until it doesn't.

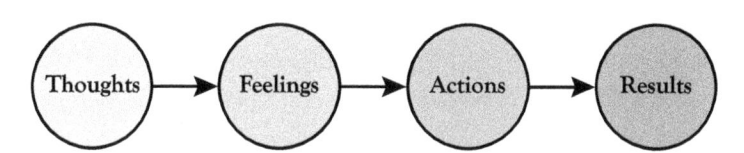

Figure 2.2 The psychology of achievement

The second thinking trap is called *thinking filters*. If you ask a person who is not color blind to focus on the color red in a room, she will have no problem finding multiple sources of red. If you change the question and ask for blue next, the assignment will remain easy. The interesting part comes when you ask her to then close her eyes and list sources of yellow in the room. Chances are that she will struggle. The reason is usually not a lack of yellow in the room. This little experiment shows something else: Our conscious mind is a goal-seeking machine. If you ask it to focus on the color red, birds in the sky or intrusive sounds, it will have no problem complying. Yet, in order to do so, it will filter out all things unrelated to the goal at hand. You won't see yellow, miss any elephants and be unaware of the low hum of the air-conditioning. Your focus will determine which thoughts you allow to enter your mind.

How to Create a Vision

Your role as a leader is therefore to put the psychology of achievement into action and get clarity on the thoughts that help achieve your goals, while at the same time preventing any thinking traps from ruining your success. Of course, this all starts with having a vision. A vision is a detailed picture in your mind of what future success would look like. A good vision can be played out in your head in the theater of the mind. It's not necessary to see this picture in your mind's eye as a blockbuster movie. Yet, it's important to get right as many details as possible. Every man-made item is based on a vision. Even the initial creator of the wooden chair must have had a picture of a chair in his mind first before cutting the first wood. This principle is true not only for building chairs, but also for designing nuclear plants, running beverage companies, and producing paper clips. In the case of the UK rowing team, the vision was simple: Increase speed and be the first to cross the finish line in the Olympics final. For engineers, it can be a bit more complicated. Yet, imagining a new bridge may still not stretch the mind too much. However, in the world of leading a business, things may become much fuzzier. What does success of a company or even team look like? Developing a clear vision in a fuzzy environment is therefore an essential activity for any effective leader.

While striving for clarity around your vision, realize that you will not see how to do it until you see yourself doing it. For example, to increase your own productivity, you need to create a vision of what increased productivity would look like. Typical questions to answer are:

- What does my ideal productive day look like?
- What kind of customers will I have?
- What kind of colleagues will I have?
- What kind of colleagues will I no longer have?
- What will I no longer do?
- What will effective meetings look like?

The next step is to realize that a vision without massive action is just a dream. To make a vision come true, it's therefore necessary to translate it into goals. This is often done in strategy documents, where a high-level vision is translated into a set of tangible goals. The problem is that getting clarity to translate a high-level vision into tangible goals often takes a lot of time, energy, and paper. I have seen companies with five-year strategy cycles along with a full year of strategy development. Since the speed of change is only accelerating, by the time the new strategy is presented, it's usually already obsolete.

How to Get Clarity on Personal Goals

How can leaders maintain speed and help translate a high-level strategic vision into medium-term tangible goals? A powerful, yet simple approach is called the *quick goal exercise*. In 60 seconds, write down your three most important goals with a horizon of 6 months to 1 year. By doing so you will have all the input needed to lead you and your organization to success. The reason is that the three goals you wrote down after doing the quick goal exercise are generated by the *subconscious* part of your brain. This part of the brain operates in the background, 24 hours per day. If, on the other hand, you would spend a week to come up with your most important three goals, you'd access the *conscious* part of your brain. This part requires active thinking: It does an idea brainstorm, looks at the existing strategic plans, makes a decision on priorities, and builds a neat spreadsheet prioritizing the most important goals.

The clarity rule around goal setting, however, is very simple: You focus on what shows up in the subconscious part of your brain. The three goals from the quick goal exercise tell you everything about your current focus. What you are focused on gets done. If you're happy with your focus, carry on! If you're unhappy, continue working on your goals until the three most important goals are imprinted on the subconscious part of your brain. How do you know it's there? This is called the 2 a.m. test. Imagine someone wakes you up from a deep sleep at 2 a.m. in the morning and asks your three most important goals. If you can answer this question without hesitation, the goals are firmly imprinted into your subconscious (and you can go back to sleep, with the pleasant knowledge that all is well with your goal focus).

The quick goal exercise may sometimes reveal uncomfortable truths. I once worked with a company that had controlled growth as its major vision. However, when I did the quick goal exercise with the CEO, all three goals revolved around financial reporting instead of growth. It turned out the company had just undergone a major audit, which revealed several critical compliance gaps in the area of financial reporting.

How to Get Clarity on Team Goals

If you lead your team through the quick team goal exercise and ask each individual team member to write down the three most important goals for the team, you may get two different results.

One result can be that all team members write down the same goals, in the same order, using the same language. If you encounter this situation, chances are big that you are dealing with a high-performance team, with all members working together to achieve the most important common goals. This scenario, however, is rare: More often, the result is a multitude of different goals. If this happens, you are clearly not aligned as a team and need to have a leadership conversation around clarity. It starts with the question: What are we trying to achieve as a team? Only after having a conversation about this question will you decide on the three most important goals and get team alignment.

Goal alignment is an essential but often forgotten priority. Have you ever seen a group of four-year-old children playing soccer? If so, you may have noticed that the children tend to be clustered around the ball. They are also easily distracted by squirrels, hot air balloons, and ice-cream vendors, and are generally very happy when someone scores a goal somewhere. For the children, it doesn't really matter whose team scores a goal. They have loads of fun, but accomplish little. What is clearly lacking is alignment. When children grow older, they get better at alignment and start to play the game the way it is meant to be played. Interestingly enough, many professionals need to relearn the lesson of alignment to start working on the same goals in a team. Thinking in alignment is usually a strong point for engineers: All the pieces of a design puzzle must fit together in order to make any new product or process work.

Signs that alignment around the most important goals in a team is missing are:

- No discussion about individual and team goals
- Lack of transparency around individual bonus objectives of team members and the leader
- No team progress meetings focused on the most important goals
- No reporting on key performance indicators around the most important goals
- No resource sharing and collaboration among team members
- Team members can win or lose their bonus individually
- Vague language of what team success would look like

How to Get Clarity on Organizational Goals

Clarity and alignment around goals are critical to make your vision as a business leader come through. It is also important to ensure that any goal is worthy of your attention. After all, if you put energy in achieving goals, you may want to make your effort count. How do you know as a leader if your goals are meaningful, or, in other words, make the boat go faster?

Great business leaders drive business growth and therefore adopt goals aimed at growth for the entire organization. Addressing these questions will help make growth focus the core of the organization:

- Will these goals add value in the eyes of your customers? It's important to contribute and improve the condition of the customer. Keep

in mind that value can be different for you than for a customer. If, for instance, you would shorten payment terms for your customers, you may capture more value for yourself, but probably upset your customers and strain a trusting relationship. You must always strive to add value in the eyes of the people who pay your bills.
- Will these goals improve the profitability of your company? The objective of a business is to get and keep customers in a profitable way. If a goal doesn't secure or improve profitability, why are you doing it in the first place? Think about it. Did the last quality project really improve the condition of customers in a profitable way?
- Will these goals make the competition nervous? If you do what everyone else is doing, you are not distinguishing yourself from the competition and you are probably stuck. Following the herd is never a good idea as a leader. Where can you make a radical turn and do something else completely? For example, if sustainability is the current big thing, what can you do to focus on massively improving speed instead?
- Has this type of goal been achieved before? A pipe dream is a future vision that is neat, pleasant, and totally unrealistic. There is a fine line between visionary ambition and chasing pie in the sky. How would you know if you cross this line and chase a pipe dream? If this type of goal has been achieved by someone, somewhere, sometime, then go ahead. Whatever you want to achieve is possible. If this type of goal has never been achieved, then be very careful. Often, it's not the pioneers who reap the biggest rewards, but the immediate followers. Steve Jobs made Apple a lot of money by introducing a new, sleek version of an existing MP3 player: the iPod.

How to Get Clarity on Measuring Progress

A professional gambler once told me you should never count your chips on the table. He reasoned that knowing exactly how much you have won or lost may influence decision making, make you either timid or exuberant, and negatively impact your gambling success. His point was that darkness brings enlightenment. As a business leader, ignore this advice:

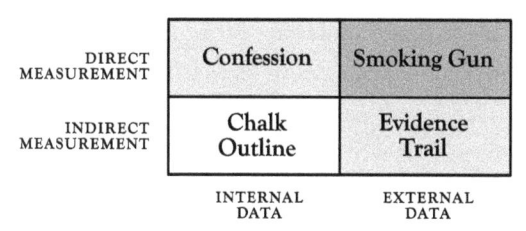

	Internal Data	External Data
Direct Measurement	Confession	Smoking Gun
Indirect Measurement	Chalk Outline	Evidence Trail

Figure 2.3 Four elements to measure goal progress

You will need the maturity to want to know exactly where you are with respect to your goals. Nothing is more dangerous than moving boldly ahead without precise understanding of your surroundings. A cruise missile receives constant feedback and adjusts course accordingly to reach its target. The two elements that determine how to measure progress on your important growth goals are which data you use to measure progress (direct versus indirect), and where you get your data on measuring progress (internal or external). Figure 2.3 shows what the four elements of progress measurement for your goals would look like.

There are four ways to measure progress on your growth goals:

- To measure progress on your growth goals directly using internal data, measure a simple number, such as market share or revenue. This direct, internal measurement is called a *confession parameter*.
- To measure progress on your growth goals directly using external data, measure customer intimacy, for example with a satisfaction score. This direct, external measurement is called a *smoking gun*.
- To measure progress on your growth goals indirectly using internal data, revert to circumstantial evidence, such as speed of innovation projects, project milestones achieved, etc. The evidence creates an outline, and this indirect, internal measurement is therefore called a *chalk outline*.
- To measure progress on your growth goals indirectly using external data, measure your innovation power, for example, by the relative amount of your patents versus the competition's. You need to go outside and follow a path littered with clues. This indirect, external measurement is therefore called a *trail of evidence*.

A spider is able to sit motionless for a long period of time, while keeping in touch with every movement in its web with only one thread. This one thread is called a *spider line*—all the feedback the spider needs to become aware of the arrival of the next meal.

Executive Question

What spider line do you need as a leader to monitor progress on your most important goals and spring into action as soon as a deviation occurs?

Why Clarity on Behaviors Is Important

You will never get the new results you want from the existing behaviors you like. Your existing mindsets and behaviors are perfectly aligned with the results you are currently getting. If you want different results, you need different behaviors. This is true for you, your team, and your organization. The UK rowing team set a new goal of winning the Olympics, identified the necessary behavioral changes as small decisions to make the boat go faster and started to make the goal happen.

As engineers, you're accustomed to processes that are often very predictable. If a process doesn't give satisfactory results, you simply tinker with parts of the process until you're satisfied. The same philosophy applies to human beings. The operating system of a human is driven by mindsets and beliefs. Mindsets and beliefs select accompanying thoughts, create feelings, drive actions, and then create results. To change the operating system of yourself and the people in your organization, you need to start with beliefs, mindsets, and especially behaviors. The reason is that behaviors are noticeable by outsiders and can be changed. For example, think back 20 years ago and consider which of your fundamental beliefs have changed and how this change has influenced your current behaviors. If you have trouble recalling your thinking from 20 years ago, see if you can find an old diary or calendar. You will be astonished by what you find.

As a boardroom consultant and business leader, I have seen dozens of elaborate strategies to achieve goals. The best ones tend to cover clear goals, organizational alignment, realistic assumptions, and progress measurements. Very seldom, however, do they cover the most important topic: behaviors. For any strategy to be successful, there is one question that is almost always missing: Which behaviors will be most helpful to achieve the strategy in the easiest, fastest, and most elegant way possible? In Chapter 5, we will discuss this question in more detail. For now, it's important to realize that you're not only a leader, but a role model as well. As a role model, you set clear standards in an organization, not only for performance, but especially for behaviors. The minimum effective behaviors you demonstrate yourself as a leader are the maximum effective behaviors you can expect from others.

Summary and What's Next

This chapter has shown that, as a business leader, it's essential to have a vision: a clear idea of what you want to achieve. In order to make this vision happen, you need to translate this vision into goals. To achieve goals, you need to make a connection with others. The best way to build this connection is to engage the subconscious part of the brain, which has to be done with clear personal goals, clear team goals, and clear organizational goals. Finally, it's important to get clarity on your spider line—how will you measure progress on your goals—and on the new behaviors necessary to achieve your goals.

Now that we have discussed clarity around your goals, we will take the next step and turn to Part III of this book: focus. In the next chapter, we will cover how to apply your unique strengths, as derived from your engineering training, to focus on the most important mindsets, behaviors, and skills to achieve your big goals.

PART III

Even Michael Jordan Plays a Lousy Basketball Game in the Dark

CHAPTER 3

Engineering Strengths

How do you build on your unique strengths as a leader with an engineering background to achieve your goals?

Why Developing Strengths Matters

Recently, a senior operations executive shared with me his biggest frustration with his talented engineers. He lamented that every time his high-potential engineers joined a business meeting with senior leaders, they ended up with a list of action points. They acted like overpaid message boys. He wished they would stop running errands, start pushing back on nonsensical ideas and really behave like peers.

Listening to the voice of the customer is all the rage in modern business leadership, but what about the voice of the engineer? The good news is that in business, there are many examples of engineers stepping up to develop leadership skills and become accomplished business leaders. The traditional approach to improve leadership performance is to focus on teaching engineers more business acumen, for example with an MBA. This often includes developing more soft skills, like active listening, servant leadership, and inclusive teamwork. This plan explains the myriad courses to improve human interaction skills, ranging from becoming more adept at public speaking, to more esoteric forms of training, such as horse listening.

The idea that engineers are held back from becoming effective business leaders because of limited soft skills and emotional quotient (EQ), is a myth. Engineers are not damaged and don't need fixing in the soft skill department. The reason is that if you focus on developing additional soft skills, you don't build on traditional engineering strengths. Instead of becoming an excellent business leader, you run the risk of creating a mediocre human resources (HR) professional. To quote Mark Twain, "Never try to teach a pig to sing. It wastes your time and annoys the pig."

Instead, the secret to becoming a great business leader with an engineering background is to simply focus on your unique strengths and at the same time get rid of unhelpful habits that mask these strengths. Take for example Alan Mulally. Trained as an aeronautical engineer, the former CEO of Ford has been credited for turning around the struggling Ford Motor Company between 2005 and 2014. What made him enormously effective was his no-nonsense leadership style, focused on a process called *the business process review* (BPR). In the weekly BPR, Mulally systematically reviewed key indicators—his spider line—of the Ford company with his senior executives. Mulally's process-oriented approach to leadership proved to be enormously effective to refocus the company on what really mattered.

There are two mechanisms to enforce the mistaken attitude that engineering strengths should be reduced in importance and that damage control by carefully building more soft skills is the best road for engineers to become more effective leaders:

- *The Superman stereotype.* Hollywood emphasizes that if you simply drop your Kent Clark glasses, a superhero will magically appear. The reality is that if you drop your glasses, it's more likely you will stumble into a wall.
- *The peak performance fallacy.* The thinking is that, since engineers are so good at mathematics, processes, and solution-based thinking, there is not much to learn here. Let's focus on holding inclusive deep listening circles instead.

To accelerate your career, don't necessarily focus on soft skills, but on boosting your strengths and getting rid of unhelpful habits. You will find more about getting rid of adverse habits in Chapter 8.

Why All-Round Leadership Excellence Is a Myth

Three cardinal rules are important for exceptional business leaders when they focus on building on strengths.

The first is that it is much easier to build on strengths than to compensate weaknesses. This is only natural, as we need far less energy to become twice as strong in areas where we are already strong than to try to become 10 percent stronger in areas where we are weak. For example, the exemplary violin player Yehudi Menuhin was able to reach additional peak performance by a never-ending routine of violin practice. He probably would have been a lousy nuclear engineer, even if he had used all of his training effort to become proficient in mathematics and physics. Before you dismiss this example as silly, you have to realize that this bizarre approach to people development is common practice in many organizations. Take the standard performance review. Odds are that the vast majority of time is spent discussing your weaknesses or "development opportunities" instead of your strengths. The idea that you grow by compensating your weaknesses is simply wrong. Great business leaders know that if you spend a lifetime compensating your weaknesses, you end with a large set of strong weaknesses. This practice is a recipe for mediocrity, not for extraordinary achievement.

The second rule is that the more profound your abilities, the more profound your weaknesses. The reason is very simple. It takes a lot of time to develop massively strong skills. The popular thinking is that it takes 10,000 hours to become a master. Though this number is often disputed, the point remains the same. The time spent building strengths was not spent learning other things. If knowledge and abilities are deep, they lack width. This theory explains why Einstein was lousy at relationships, Ernest Hemingway repeatedly lost large sums of money, and the late Steve Jobs had questionable judgment regarding his own health and vitality.

The third rule is that profound abilities and strengths will float to the surface when behaviors that mask strengths are eliminated. It's not uncommon to read stories about individuals, in bad physical condition, who decide to get serious about health and end up running marathons. At the same time, they also started to exhibit great success in their chosen professions or careers. The behaviors that masked their strengths were eliminated so strengths can bloom.

Thus, successful business leaders do not possess all-round excellence, but are able to achieve extraordinary success by spiking their strengths even further. What strengths do leaders with an engineering background typically have, that can be applied to achieve big-growth goals?

How to Recognize Your Super-Talents

Everyone has talents. Some are reasonably good at organizing stuff, at mathematics, or at languages. However, everyone also has super-talents. What is interesting about super-talents is that we are so good at them, we don't consciously recognize our own talents. In other words, the behaviors and thinking patterns associated with these super-talents come so natural to us that it's very difficult to imagine anyone else struggling. It's like riding a bike. Once you get it, muscle memory takes over and balance becomes natural.

How do you recognize your own super-talents? There are some glaring clues.

First of all, you turn to your super-talents when faced with obstacles and difficulties. When cyclist Lance Armstrong was diagnosed with cancer, he applied his super-talent, his unbelievable discipline, to rigorously adopt a regime that would make him healthy again. He conquered cancer, but in the end his super-talent became a two-edged sword. He became so obsessed with winning that he turned to illegal drugs to win the Tour de France.

Second, other people come to you to get advice about your super-talent. As a professional speaker, I often receive spontaneous requests to critique the speaking of others.

Third, you love to be immersed in the subject of your super-talent. If you are good at strategic business thinking, I'll bet your library has books like *The Art of War* and *The Effective Executive*. This interest and even obsession fuels you super-talent. The more you engage with understanding the intricate details of your obsession, the better you will perform.

As an engineer, you may not notice your own super-talents. In my work with thousands of professionals with an engineering background, I have noticed, however, that three talents are common in almost all of them: reality-based thinking, process design, and accelerated learning.

Why Reality-Based Thinking Matters

The first strength of an engineer is reality-based thinking. As profound management thinker Peter Drucker once noticed, "What's the reality?" might be the most important question in business. Hope is not a strategy.

Reality-based thinking has several components. The first is the ability to make *decisions driven by data*. For example, once you realize that wind turbines are running at capacity less than 40 percent of the time, you understand that wind energy will never be a viable and cheap solution for more conventional forms of energy production, unless cheap ways of massive energy storage are developed as well. An effective business leader is able to not only sell an idea, but also to bring that idea to a successful conclusion. This skill separates engineers from other professionals, such as trend watchers, politicians, and futurists. These professionals don't need to be concerned with how things work out in the end. The sale of their idea is the most important part of their success. This truth explains why people continue to turn to the predictions of stock market investment gurus, although history has shown the reliability of many of these predictions is typically worse than that of Tarot cards, hand reading, or astrology.

The second component of reality-based thinking is the ability to *clarify assumptions*. Assumptions are the underlying laws, convictions, or ideas that support a course of action. For instance, many budget predictions are based on the assumption that the economy continues to grow at its current pace. There is nothing wrong with working with assumptions. After all, life would be unlivable without the assumption that the sun will rise tomorrow. However, when key assumptions are not brought to the surface, things may go pear-shaped rapidly. We therefore need not only to press for clarity about our assumptions, but also to have a system in place to check these assumptions on a regular basis.

The third component of reality-based thinking is the ability to *overcome systematic thinking biases*. An example of a notorious systematic thinking bias is *self-selecting bias*. For example, if you would ask the greatest minds in economy if economic forecasts are relevant and reliable, you will probably get a resounding *yes*. It would be a mistake to take this opinion as the best there is though. After all, economists have spent lifetimes becoming masters of their professions. Naturally, any conclusion that diminishes these efforts would be met with hostility. As Upton Sinclair once noticed: "It is difficult to get a man to understand something when his salary depends upon his not understanding it." To overcome self-selecting bias, a good question for a leader to subject experts is therefore: what needs to happen to dismiss your conclusion or prediction? If no answer can be given, you are not dealing with science, but with superstition.

This doesn't mean that the role of the leader should be an endless quest to gather more information. In this case, action paralysis ensures that nothing will happen. The role of the leader is to always be curious to find different ways to understand reality and take action on the available data.

To sharpen your effectiveness, it's therefore essential to be data-driven, aware of assumptions, and always alert to thinking biases. It doesn't mean that intuition will not play a role. Making a decision by definition involves both hard data and your intuition. After all, you will never have all the information available. How can reality-based thinking help to improve decision-making?

How to Apply Reality-Based Thinking

Engineers are pragmatists, trained to keep on testing and questioning until the feedback from reality gives satisfactory results. The ability to make the right business decisions in the face of uncertainty is called *executive judgment*. The world grows more complex every day, and well-developed judgment skills are in short supply. The twin engines that drive good executive judgment when choosing between different options are feasibility and effectiveness. Figure 3.1 shows the impact of feasibility and effectiveness on the quality of judgment.

If a course of action is neither effective nor feasible, you are operating in the pleasant land of *magical thinking*. This is where the quality of a good story trumps the unpleasant boundaries of reality. An example of magical thinking is the business case to cover a huge area in the Sahara Desert with solar cells, to make energy almost free and abundant. With the current state of technology, this thinking is neither feasible (it requires a stunning amount of resources) nor effective (how do you

ENGINEERING STRENGTHS   39

```
                    HIGH FEASIBILITY
                          ↑
         Symbolic Thinking | Reality-based Thinking
  LOW                      |                    HIGH
  EFFECTIVENESS  ←─────────┼─────────→  EFFECTIVENESS
         Magical Thinking  | Utopian Thinking
                          ↓
                    LOW FEASIBILITY
```

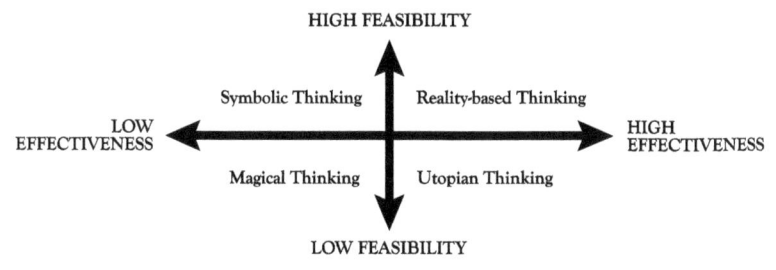

Figure 3.1 The impact of feasibility and effectiveness on the quality of executive judgment

produce energy in the night?). Yet, despite these massive obstacles, many (political) leaders still pour abundant resources into these types of unicorn projects.

If a course of action is feasible but lacks effectiveness, you tend to focus on *symbolic thinking* instead of substance. The key question to determine effectiveness for a business leader is therefore "Will this course of action bring us closer to our most important goals?" If yes, make it happen. If no, apply ruthless judgment to move on. How bold can you be in your thinking? Don't waste time on symbolic, half-hearted actions. Teaching cannibals how to eat with knife and fork is hardly progress.

If an option is effective but not feasible, you deal with *utopian thinking*. When Volkswagen decided to become the biggest carmaker in the world, its greatest roadblock was to make sure its diesel engines would meet ever-stricter environmental requirements at a low cost. Since this goal was technically impossible, the engineers were cajoled into installing a so-called defeat device: a program that recognizes an emission test cycle and consequently adjusts an engine to run in a non-representative testing mode to meet emission standards. When federal regulators became aware of this illegal device in 2015, the resulting fines for the company were massive and the carmaker's ambition to become number one hit a serious roadblock. The question to test feasibility is, "Has it been done before?" If not, risks are high, and you may reconsider whether the huge effort to become a pioneer is better used elsewhere.

Only when decisions are based on effectiveness and feasibility, is judgment grounded in *reality-based thinking*. Reality-based judgment is an intuitive skill for almost every engineer. After all, engineers are used to dealing with reality all the time. Since they are focused on building things in the real world, lack of proper judgment may literally bring the house down. Excellent business leaders are able to translate intuitive judgment skills to the fine art of decision making in business areas as well. The two elements of judgment—effectiveness and feasibility—codify how the best decisions are being made. Once you know how to apply reality-based thinking to improve judgment successfully, you have the ability to enhance this skill even further and become a better leader in the process.

Why Process Design Matters

The second strength of an engineer is process design. A process is a sequence of steps to get a desired outcome. Processes are vital to a well-run organization because:

- The only way to get repeatable results is through a process. This is the reason checklists are used widely in the medical field and aviation.
- They help to get not only results, but especially favorable results for the organization.
- There is method to the madness for almost any business activity. Applying a proven process usually skips a long and painful learning curve.
- They save a lot of time. Why invent the wheel when the wheel blueprint is readily available?
- They eliminate mistakes. A start-up safety checklist in a chemical plant provides a guarantee that the essential safety measures are in place before starting up.
- They get predictable results. The last things you are looking for when designing a bridge are risks and uncertainties.
- They are scalable. FedEx developed a spoke-and-hub-system to get overnight delivery. The company started with a few test packages, and as soon as it was successful, it simply increased the numbers.
- They are transferrable to other areas. An autopilot function on a plane has much in common with an autopilot function on a train.

The aptitude to apply logic to build processes is the hallmark of an engineering education. This aptitude is how chemical plants, automobiles, and computer chips are built and new leadership approaches are developed. What is true for engineering is true for leadership as well. Leadership is about getting results. Why not apply process thinking to parts of a business outside the field of engineering? If you don't have a process to achieve a certain result, you are at the mercy of someone else's process for providing that result.

A fascinating example can be found in sales. If you want to grow your company, you need to realize that if you do not have a process for selling, you rely on someone else's process for buying. Selling is an almost scientific process and should not depend on chance. This fact is especially important for business leaders, since sales drive growth, supplying the life blood of any business. One of the most important steps in the sales process happens after a sale is made. Especially for professional services, this moment is when referrals can be harvested. These referrals will fuel the start of a new sales cycle. Unless you have a systematic sales process, it is unlikely you will have a systematic referral process to fuel future growth.

An important task of a business leader is therefore to codify existing processes for key business functions, such as sales, strategy, and innovation. Once you understand an existing process, you will be able to improve upon this process. No structural improvement is possible without understanding the method to the madness.

This design thinking is not limited to business processes. It can be equally applied to shape behaviors and build a high-performance culture. Although you can't predict with 100 percent certainty how people will behave, you can systematically vary your own leadership behaviors to get the desired results. This is called *systematic behavior testing*. You continue to test different approaches to get different results. As a child, many have had ample experience with this approach. If we wanted to get candy and crying wouldn't help, you would turn to begging, or more sophisticated forms of persuasion.

By adopting a systematic approach to achieving a desired result, business leaders with an engineering background play to their strengths. Earlier you saw Alan Mulally applied process thinking to steer right behaviors in the Ford Motor Company.

How to Apply Process Design

A process can either be *engineered* or *reverse engineered*. If it is engineered, you typically start from scratch and build the interlinking pieces from there. This is why there are best practices around project management, giving feedback, and balanced scorecards.

If something has been reverse engineered, you start with an example of a desirable result and work backward to understand how you arrived at this result—a popular method of many modern management thinkers. Think of best sellers like *Built to last*, which looks at key characteristics of top performers and distills the essential part for others to become high performers as well. The problem, of course, is that with reverse engineering, you may confuse correlation with causation. The sun doesn't rise because of the rooster crowing in the morning. This way of thinking explains why, less than 20 years after its publication, many companies identified in *Built to Last* have fallen from grace.

Despite these concerns, there are two major applications of reverse engineering for business leaders. First, reverse engineering is an invaluable tool for strategic goal-achieving. In other words, begin with the end in mind and then go back to identify the necessary steps to achieve the results. Second, it's a powerful approach to innovate and find hidden gems and opportunities. For example, Viagra was originally conceived as a treatment for heart disease. That didn't work. However, while studying its side effects, Pfizer marketeers got a very different and very successful idea for its use.

Executive Question

One of the most important questions to drive innovation is to ask as a leader: What should not work, but is working anyway? How can you apply reverse engineering to systematically obtain more of these excellent results?

Why Accelerated Learning Matters

The third engineering strength is accelerated learning. In 2015, an artificial intelligence (AI) computer program called AlphaGo defeated the human world champion of the board game Go. Go is a deceptively simple game that actually is so complex that it's impossible for any computer to evaluate enough possible scenarios of different moves in real time to play at a high level. Rather than relying on massive processing power, AlphaGo, therefore, focused on one thing: practice. AlphaGo continued to play against itself for months, using up to 30 million preloaded moves to apply accelerated learning and develop game-winning strategies on its own.

With the pace of technological and scientific progress accelerating, it's obvious that successful business leaders need to accelerate their learning as well. Accelerated learning is defined by the speed, frequency, and size (or depth) of the feedback. Figure 3.2 shows the relationship between different forms of feedback and accelerated learning.

If feedback of an action is fast and frequent but lacks size or depth, learning is *shallow*. If, for instance, you try to learn a foreign language by mindlessly repeating sentences from an audiobook, you will gradually improve. Since this method does not require deep learning by building sentences yourself, improvements will be shallow.

If feedback of an action is fast and sizable but is not very frequent, you tend to learn *slowly*. Think of the space shuttle program, where learning was limited by the low frequency of launch events.

If feedback of an action is frequent and sizable but lacks speed, you deal with *delayed learning*. This challenge, for example, occurs with the massive particle collider in Switzerland (CERN), where any quantum

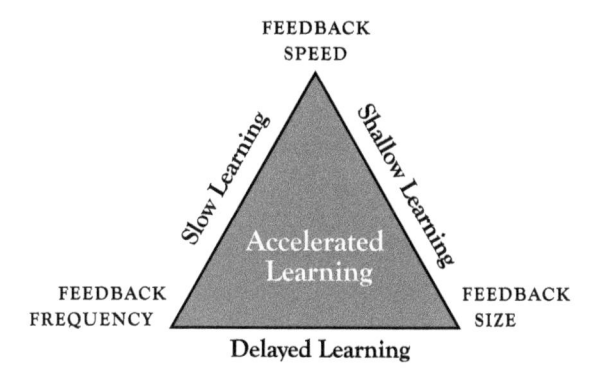

Figure 3.2 The effect of different forms of feedback on accelerated learning

experiment generally lasts a very short period of time but produces a massive amount of data that may take years to be interpreted.

Thus, accelerated learning only happens when feedback from actions and experiments is fast, frequent, and significant. In engineering terms, this result is called *flash testing*. The design and execution of small pilots for flash testing are powerful tools in the engineering toolbox.

Good examples of the smart application of accelerated learning are the actions of the carmaker Volvo. Volvo is famous for its focus on safety. Since 1969, a dedicated team investigates every Volvo crash in Sweden. Its aim is to learn as much as possible from real-world accidents. In 2000, under the guidance of CEO Leif Eriksson, the carmaker stepped up its game and opened a state-of-the-art and unique car crash facility. This facility provided even more speedy, frequent, and significant feedback to help the carmaker improve the safety of its cars further and stay on top of its game.

Flash testing is not limited to the lab. Excellent leaders apply this approach to rapidly become better as an organization as well. For example, while building a high-performance culture in a large global company, our team applied a behavioral survey to test any improvements after each company-wide engagement. The results of this fast, frequent, and impactful feedback helped us do more of what worked and quickly get rid of what didn't work. There were no failures, only outcomes of tests.

Executive Question

How can you design and apply quick pilots with fast, sizeable, and frequent feedback, to accelerate learning for you and your organization?

How to Apply Accelerated Learning

A lawyer who becomes an engineer is very rare. An engineer who becomes a patent lawyer is, however, quite common. What would explain this uneven balance? One explanation is that engineering is maybe boring, and becoming skilled at this discipline is not really worth the time and effort. Of course, I propose a different explanation. It's fairly easy for an engineer to become proficient in another professional skill. The reason is that a large part of an engineering education is to learn how to learn.

This approach to learning expresses itself in various forms. First, *pattern recognition* is a powerful tool in the area of problem solving. After all, once you identify a problem, you don't have to reinvent the wheel when faced with a different yet similar problem. If you recognize the pattern when learning different skills, it's easy to apply and adopt this pattern to become better quickly. For example, an effective presentation adheres to certain standard patterns.

Practical Application

One powerful pattern for an effective presentation is to answer three questions:

- What do you want the audience to *know?*
- How do you want the audience to *feel?*
- What do you want the audience to *do?*

Applying this simple know-feel-do pattern will massively improve the persuasion skills of any leader.

Second, *natural laws* and *rules of thumb* quickly become your friend. The Romans mastered the secrets to building arches to support heavy roofs. The old Roman temples, still standing, are a testament to their craft, and these practices have been used by their successors for hundreds of years. Learning a new practice opens the door to thousands of possibilities. Just like pattern recognition, rules of thumb and natural laws are cause-and-effect relations, often put on paper.

Finally, reality-based thinking provides powerful feedback from reality and enables the engineer to keep on testing until the desired result is met. The translation from the theoretical to the practical is a humbling experience. Looking for feedback is not always natural. It can be a brutal experience, yet nature cannot be fooled.

Pattern recognition, natural laws, and feedback from reality ensure learning patterns that are fast and effective, and can be applied broadly to other business skills. This provides a leader with an engineering background with agility to effectively deal with a changing world. For example, advertising is nothing more than the application of the science of persuasion. It consists of three main ingredients:

Ingredient 1: Pattern recognition. The story of the product or service is often set up with the *hero's journey template* of storytelling.
1. Once upon a time there was . . .
2. Every day . . .
3. One day . . .
4. Because of that . . .
5. Because of that . . .
6. Until finally . . .

Ingredient 2: Rule of thumb. People are most fond of what they cannot have. If you suggest scarcity of a product, it will therefore be more coveted.

Ingredient 3: Flash testing. The effectiveness of a product advertising campaign is often tested with an A/B split. A magazine has two print runs. One run contains advertisement A, the other contains a different advertisement B for the same product. The best advertisement is the one with the highest response rate.

Table 3.1 gives an overview of engineering strengths, how these strengths translate to leadership skills and behaviors, and the main applications of these strengths in business.

Table 3.1 The relation between engineering strengths, leadership skills and behaviors, and business application

Engineering strengths	Leadership skills and behaviors	Business application
Reality-based thinking	• Data-driven decisions • Clarify assumptions • Overcome thinking biases	Executive judgment based on feasibility and effectiveness
Process design	Codify key business processes by engineering or reverse engineering	• Strategy execution: begin with the end in mind • Innovation: what's working despite of everything
Accelerated learning	Agility by actively looking for feedback	Expanding skills by: • Pattern recognition • Rules of thumb • Feedback from reality

Where to Deploy Your Strengths

Now that you've discovered the three strengths of engineers—reality-based thinking, process design, and accelerated learning—the question is where to deploy these strengths to become better business leaders. For this, let's take a closer look at a different field: long-term investing in the stock market.

Successful long-term investing in the stock market is guided by two universal rules:

- Risk and reward are correlated. The higher the risk, the higher the potential rewards. For example, investing in questionable loans (junk-bonds) may result in huge profits, but may also expose you to massive losses.
- In order to optimize results, it's important to build a portfolio balanced with high-risk assets (to maximize gains) and low-risk assets (to minimize losses). Ideally, the two asset classes should have a low correlation. For example, if your portfolio consists of both stocks and bonds, the stocks part will perform well in a growing market (bull market) and the bonds part will perform well in a shrinking market (bear market). This approach is called *portfolio thinking*. The most important decision for portfolio thinking is therefore asset allocation: the distribution between risky assets (in this case stocks) and less risky assets (in this case bonds). The best asset allocation for an individual investor depends on many factors, such as risk tolerance and age.

The example of the two rules for successful investing in the stock market can be applied to becoming great business leader. In order to grow as a leader, you need to apply part of your strengths to more risky endeavors. To mitigate the downside of this risk, you need to apply the remaining part of your strengths to more safer endeavors.

What is a safe endeavor? Generally speaking, a safe endeavor is to perform well at your current job. For example, if you are an operations manager in a large organization, delivering products within budget and time and according to specifications, will create essential value to your organization. You manage the running business. It doesn't mean that risk is completely mitigated, as you may still lose your job if the company hits a wall. It means, however, that if you apply the skills that are immediately applicable to your current role, you continue to create value, and you become better by gradually building experience. This is called working *in* your job, or *in* your business: you are slowly becoming better at what you are responsible for right now.

Let's now focus on more risky endeavors. These are activities with a much higher reward and constitute working *on* your job, or *on* your business. As you've seen, the best activities to make massive gains have two characteristics: they are focused on business growth, and they make plentiful use of the power laws. As discussed earlier, a power law describes how small differences can yield exponential results. In business, only three activities incorporate the power laws to massively improve growth: marketing, innovation, and strategy.

Marketing includes activities to help attract the best customers to your company. Think of white papers, advertisements, social media, client knowledge sessions, etc.

Innovations improve the value you create for your clients in a profitable way by doing things differently. This value is not limited to product innovation, but extends to areas like service improvement as well. Think of improving delivery speed or extending product service.

Strategy encompasses activities to help you achieve big goals in the easiest way possible. Strategy can be as big as a merger, or as small as systematically building appropriate leadership behaviors.

Marketing, innovation, and strategy are the only business activities that make ample use of the power laws. They don't have a ceiling if they are effectively applied. For example, if you improve logistics and increase production speed for a client, the effect may resonate through your entire business. On the other hand, if you focus on a business activity that cannot leverage the power laws, say cost cutting, you will quickly reach a ceiling. In this case, the ceiling is, of course, zero.

How to Drive Growth Goals

As a business leader, it's important to allocate your strengths and create the right balance between working in your business and working on your business. Figure 3.3 illustrates this balance.

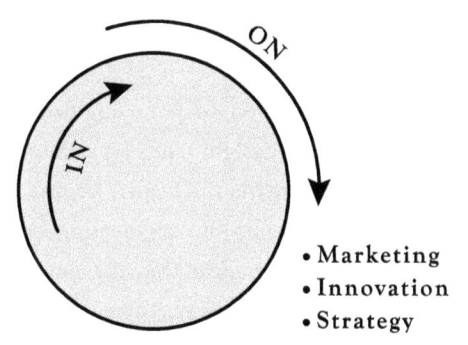

Figure 3.3 Working-in versus working-on your business

The allocation between working in and working on your business has major applications for your ability as a leader to achieve big goals. Imagine that 90 percent of your energy is dedicated to working in your business, which is maintaining the running business. The remaining 10 percent is dedicated to working on your business. Now imagine that, as a business leader, your focus on applying your strengths to business growth enables you to shift your energy from 90 percent working in the business, to 80 percent working in the business. Since marketing, innovation, and strategy activities increase to 20 percent, your activities focused on achieving growth goals simply double. A small shift in your leadership focus can therefore massively increase the speed to achieve ambitious growth goals. The simple act of setting growth goals and focusing your three unique engineering strengths to marketing, innovation, and strategy will therefore have a huge impact on your effectiveness as a business leader.

Thinking back to risk versus reward and asset allocation, the similarities of long-term investing success in the stock market and business leadership development become clear. If you only work in your job, the low-risk part of your portfolio is expanded. You simply become better at what you do every single day to maintain the running business part of your job. Typically, over time you will take a deep dive in a narrowly defined profession. If you work on your job and extend activities and allocate time to marketing, sales, and strategy to focus on growth, you will broaden your leadership skills and invest in the growth part of your career. Talent allocation therefore means using your strengths to find the balance between doing your current job well and preparing for your next job by driving business growth.

How can you use the allocation of your engineering strengths—reality-based thinking, process design, and accelerated learning—to extend your job and focus on marketing, sales, or strategy? Here's an example. Once while I was leading an engineering department in a Fortune 1000 company, it became clear that the new company strategy required different leadership behaviors. I decided to use two of my strengths—process design and accelerated learning—to support the company strategy. I did so by creating workshops to help employees identify and adopt new behaviors to build a high-performance organization. I devised a simple system to build new habits and used the quick feedback mechanism of accelerated learning to make the new behaviors stick. I became a widely sought-after company speaker and trainer, and before long I got a new job: driving the overall strategy to build a high-performance organization.

Summary and What's Next

This chapter has demonstrated that successful business leaders do not possess all-round excellence, but are able to achieve extraordinary success by spiking their strengths even further and eliminating unhelpful behaviors that mask strengths. The three strengths of engineers—reality-based thinking, process design, and accelerated learning—can be used to quickly expand your skills to areas other than engineering. Doing so requires a shift in focus from working in your business to working on your business. In practice, this shift means that, regardless of your position in an organization, applying your strengths to support marketing, innovation, and strategy are essential to achieving big growth goals and improve as a business leader.

However, while applying your strengths to support business growth, you will undoubtedly face obstacles. The next chapter will therefore discuss how to use your engineering talents to overcome adversity while walking the path to achieving your goals.

External Perspective

Interview Luca Rosetto, Senior VP Operations, DSM Nutritional Products

What Has Been the Most Fascinating Aspect of Business Leadership for You?

That would be dealing with people, which is both fascinating and at the same time, the most difficult part of business leadership. When I got my first leadership position, leading a quality control lab, it was both scary and exciting. During the first part of my career, I could count on my own knowledge and capabilities; now I had to learn how to get results through people. No formal scientific or other education will train you for this: you need to learn by doing. Success would require learning agility and curiosity. A key element is that you need to develop a good insight into yourself and your own values first. Only then will you be able to understand what makes other people tick. This self-examination enables you to build on strengths and on what drives other people.

Since they often work in manufacturing environments that employ lots of people, engineers often get the chance to lead large groups at young ages. This experience is a big advantage, since you tend to learn most when you are younger. They quickly learn to turn the classic organizational pyramid upside down. In the end, the operators are the owners of the process, and effective manufacturing leaders focus on creating a supporting environment where operators can do their best work. These leaders create the right *smell of the place*.

What Are Some of the Biggest Myths about Leaders with Engineering Background?

First, it's a myth that only your formal education will somehow determine your success. Your success is determined by your agility, ability to connect and learn, curiosity, and knowing yourself. These attitudes will break through any mental stiffness. It's true that you learn most from your own mistakes. This truth is often harsh, but it's very powerful.

(continued)

You learn a lot about yourself from the reactions of others. For this reason, it's so important to be authentic. If you hide behind an image, you will get feedback on that image instead of on your real self. For leaders, it's therefore essential to create time to rewind. For example, I block time in my agenda to reflect. I also have the habit of being in the office between 7:15 and 7:30 a.m., when the office is still a quiet place. There are very few interruptions, which helps me reflect. I'm happiest when I look back at yesterday and realize that I would have done some things differently if I could do it over again. I feel no regret, because it means I continue to learn and grow, and makes what I do every day worthwhile and exciting.

Second, it's a myth that your scientific background provides some kind of rigid thinking structure. On the contrary, it provides a flexible structure to quickly reach synthesis. It's not true that your education lacks deep thinking, because it's focused on solving the problems of today. Your scientific mind provides a curiosity to learn and a strategy to build the future. This drive for the unknown actually stimulates long-term thinking.

CHAPTER 4

Overcoming Obstacles

How can you use your unique engineering strengths to anticipate and overcome obstacles on the way to achieving your goals?

Why Overcoming Obstacles Matters

Many great initiatives and big ambitions start with gusto but fade away somewhere along the road to success. Most of us are familiar with new year's resolutions. The start of a new year inspires many to think of and define new initiatives, set new goals, and make bold promises: This time it's going to be different. Most of us are also familiar with what comes next: Somehow we lose momentum, dilute our focus, and quietly give up. At the start of the following year, we will dust up our old ambitions and simply start anew.

This recurring story is not limited to personal goals, but is seen in business as well. A huge corporate initiative takes center stage and is broadly communicated. Top executives line up to declare their support and the organization gets going. However, at a certain point in time, the initiative falters. Here are typical warning signs of imminent failure:

- **Reverse countdown:** What was agenda point number one in every meeting now slowly moves to the number two spot and rapidly slides further down the ladder as time passes.
- **Hallway lip service:** In the beginning, the new initiative is boldly brought up in meaningful conversations usually starting with "How can we . . .," or "What about . . . ?" Then the language changes to "Does anyone has anything to say about . . . ?"

Hedgehog reflex: Whenever the big initiative is brought up, leaders ball up like a frightened hedgehog. Mentioning it is lauded extensively (thank you for bringing this up) and is immediately followed by the reflexive (but, we first have to focus on . . .).

Work under a different banner: A new supreme leader armed with new ideas and priorities is brought in, and bold initiatives from predecessors are frowned upon.

Information graveyard: The flashy website is no longer updated, newsletters cease to be distributed, and all written material is at least a year old.

Restart button: A second new initiative is launched, usually branded as building on the success of the previous one. Insiders know better. The old initiative is dead, and long live the new one.

Looking at the landscape of bold initiatives that fade away like a faint candle, you recognize that governments, companies, and professionals suffer from a consistent pattern that often leads to failure. This pattern is called the *Valley of Death*. Figure 4.1 describes the Valley of Death: the relationship among enthusiasm, time, and goal-achieving.

The Valley of Death describes what happens with your enthusiasm between the first moment you have a vision of a new goal and the final moment where you achieve this goal in the real world. When you are first hit with a good idea, you get excited and life looks rosy. You start sharing your ideas with others and they get excited too. This is contagious and your energy level goes up even further. When you start to work on the

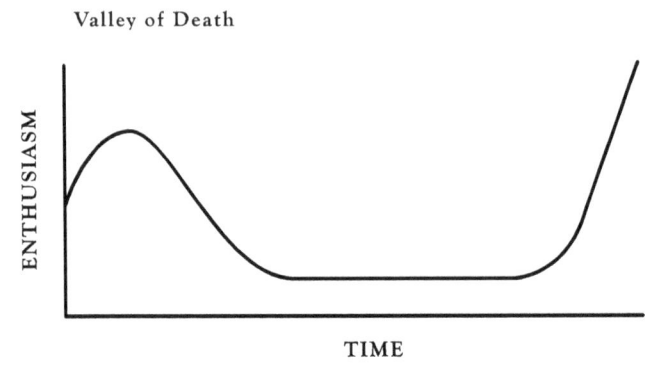

Figure 4.1 The Valley of Death

goal, things go downhill from there. Progress is slow, others become less supportive, and at a certain point in time you reach a low-level enthusiasm plateau. This point is where many initiatives are abandoned. Only after you have persisted and crossed this plateau does your success become inevitable and your energy and enthusiasm resurge. The persistence to cross the Valley of Death is necessary for leaders who want to become experts at goal-achieving.

Why Ignoring the Valley of Death Is Dangerous

The bigger and bolder the goal, the longer and deeper the Valley of Death will be. This makes sense: The Valley of Death for developing a new software application is shorter and shallower than the Valley of Death to bring a man to Mars. Big goals require overcoming big obstacles. This is actually good news: If you don't face big obstacles, you are probably not thinking big enough.

The curious thing, however, is that in many corporate environments, the Valley of Death is simply ignored and the initial planning is presented as a straight, unhindered line from A to B. Figure 4.2 illustrates this strange phenomenon.

Unfortunately, ignoring the Valley of Death and presenting a corporate fantasy instead is often driven by the *planning fallacy*. The planning fallacy is a thinking bias in which we consistently underestimate the time and effort required to get a project done. There are many examples of the planning fallacy. The new Berlin airport was supposed to be ready by

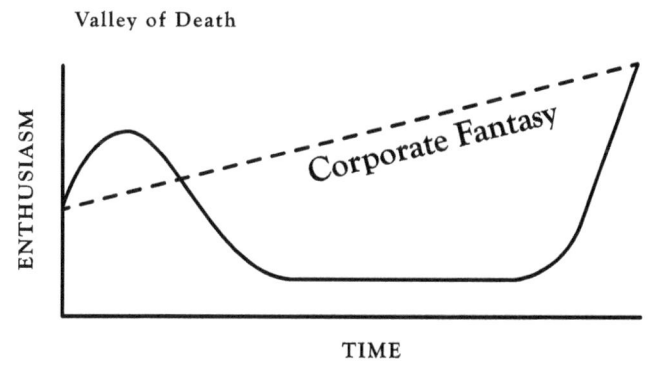

Figure 4.2 Corporate fantasy and the Valley of Death

2011. At the time of this writing (2018), the airport is still not ready and is facing a cost overrun of almost 400 percent. A practical way to overcome the planning fallacy is *baseline thinking*. Use data of similar projects as a baseline for your planning and then move up or down based on your skills and competences. Baseline thinking, of course, makes ample use of your strength as an engineer: reality-based thinking.

When crossing the Valley of Death it's important to distinguish between a goal and an activity. A goal requires overcoming obstacles. If there are no obstacles on your way to achieving a goal, then it's not a goal, but simply an activity: a straight line from A to B which can be done by everybody. For example, reaching your office is an activity. Reaching your office every day at 7 a.m. for the entire year is a goal. If you confuse the two and think only in activities, you will seriously diminish your potential. After all, a good goal should be stretched to the point of your slight discomfort.

Why New Initiatives Often Fail

Why is it that the plateau of the Valley of Death resembles the graveyard of good ideas, great initiatives, and boundless ambition? In my experience, the answer is procrastination. Procrastination means that you need to do something, you're not doing it, and you feel miserable about it. Procrastination is the thief of time and it's the main reason why it's difficult to follow through on achieving a new goal. To overcome procrastination, you need to understand where it comes from.

For this, let's turn to a simplified model of the human brain. This model tells us we have three different brains: a lizard brain, a mammalian brain, and a neocortex. The lizard brain is focused on one thing and one thing only: survival. It hates risk and uncertainty, and actually wants yesterday to look exactly like today and today to look exactly like tomorrow.

On the other side of the brain spectrum is the neocortex. Brain scientists sometimes compare this part of the brain to crazy uncle Joe who always shows up at family parties. He wants to do exciting things like bungee jumping, sky diving, and becoming a great business leader. In order to make this happen, he needs to embrace uncertainty and risk. This is the exact opposite of the objective of the lizard brain. This tug-of-war between the lizard brain and the neocortex is called *the war between your ears*.

The lizard brain is your oldest brain. Since it was there first, it has been granted veto power over your body. In other words, if it believes you will engage in risky activities, it will pull the plug and shut your body down. Hence the fact that sometimes people simply faint when they have to give an important speech. It's an effective survival mechanism. Imagine that your neocortex one day would decide it would be a good idea to see what happens if you hold your breath for more than 15 minutes. Your lizard brain would automatically kick in after two minutes and reestablish adult supervision. The problem is that the same mechanism is activated when you try to cross the Valley of Death. The siren song of the lizard brain guides you to procrastinate and even pull the plug on very important goals.

Brain scientists have identified two blunt ways of overcoming the sabotaging effects of the lizard brain. Those would be drugs and alcohol. Needless to say, these approaches aren't beneficial to your leadership style. Thus, to overcome the lizard brain, you need to apply subtle tools to unleash your neocortex and reign in your lizard brain.

The lizard brain is not limited to people, but has a collective cousin called organizational paralysis: the ability to linger in complacency and reject new thinking and ideas. It acts like a giant anchor, trying to bring any new initiative to a grinding halt. You may recognize the collective force built by many lizards in a company when:

- Most organizational energy goes to safe yet ineffective strategies to deal with big business problems. Typical examples are cost-cutting and multiple rounds of reorganizations when facing new, stiff competition in the marketplace.
- Senior leaders are more concerned with salary, bonuses, and other perks than with proposing and advancing bold ideas to serve customers better and grow the company. Buying a corporate jet is usually the first red flag.
- The most ambitious organizational project is something internal, such as a shiny new compensation system.
- Business breakthroughs don't revolve around growth and customer value, but center on payment terms, request for proposals (RFPs), and other financial gimmickry.

How to Cross the Valley of Death

To become an unstoppable goal achiever and catapult yourself deep into the ranks of the best business leaders, you need practical strategies to overcome procrastination and cross the Valley of Death. The best analogy to make that happen is again to take a page from the playbook of long-term investing in the stock market.

Long-term investing success in the stock market is determined by asset allocation, diversification between assets, and minimizing costs.

Asset allocation

Asset allocation describes the amount of money held in risky assets such as stocks and safe assets such as bonds. For example, a typical investment portfolio may consist of 70/30 allocation containing 70 percent stocks and 30 percent bonds. If stocks go down, bonds may go up, and vice versa. Thus, risk is minimized. By maintaining the desired asset allocation, investors buy stocks cheaply when the stock market is down, ensuring long-term investment success.

Diversification

Diversification tells something about how diverse the components of the different assets actually are. For example, if you have one stock of one company, you're not diversified at all, and run the risk of losing it all when this company hits a wall. On the other hand, if you own a bit of all stocks in all marketplaces, you are maximally diversified and have minimized your risk.

Costs

Cost reveals the fixed amount you lose every year for simply owning investment assets. With a long-term investment horizon of say 30 years, due to the compound effect, a cost difference of 2 percent per year on the entire investment portfolio may result in 30 percent less wealth after 30 years.

Thus, to build wealth by buying and holding investments over a long period of time with the least amount of risk, it's important to apply an investment process. Decide and stick to an asset allocation, maximize the diversification within the assets and minimize costs. The same philosophy can be applied to achieving big goals as well. In Chapter 3, we have seen how you can use the allocation of your strengths—reality-based thinking, process design, and accelerated learning—to drive business growth. By focusing on marketing, sales, and strategy, you can apply the power laws and minimize energy and costs to achieve big goals. Now, let's take a look at how diversifications and option development will help you as a leader.

Why Options Are Essential to Achieving Goals

To lull your lizard brain, it's important to reduce risk. The riskiest plans have only one route to solution. If this approach fails, the entire plan fails. Therefore, it's important to have multiple alternatives in order to achieve your goals. These alternatives are called options. They reduce risk and increase your chance of achieving your big goal. Figure 4.3 illustrates the role of options in achieving your goal.

If you want to go from A to B and have only one option to get there (the path with the multiplication sign), you get stuck if you face an obstacle. On the other hand, if there are alternative routes (the paths with the circles, pyramids, and triangles), you will be able to switch to a different option as soon as you face an insurmountable obstacle. Developing options therefore gives you freedom. If you don't have options, don't bother. It's better to use your energy elsewhere. With only one option, you have a problem. With two options, you have a dilemma. Freedom, choice, and reduction of risk arrives only when you start to cross the Valley of Death with three options or more. You diversify your plan, and the chances for success increase exponentially.

Developing options is a numbers game. It is also one of the most difficult things to do. To understand why, ask yourself a question: What is the

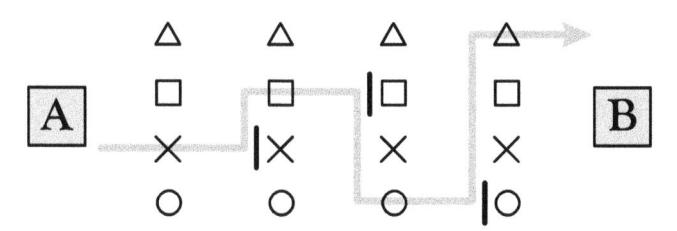

Figure 4.3 Impact of options on goal-achieving

purpose of thinking? A philosopher may have multiple answers: To live, solve problems, survive, etc. Yet a brain scientist will have only one answer: The purpose of thinking is to stop thinking. This means that thinking is a high-energy-consuming activity. People are hardwired to think in the shortest time possible so they can return to autopilot: unconscious thinking. For example, driving on autopilot is when you drive a car for 20 minutes and afterward simply can't remember anything about the drive. Scientists estimate that more than 95 percent of your life is run on autopilot. Thus, when faced with a problem you tend to think until you have something that resembles a solution. The urgency is to immediately stop thinking and turn to execution instead. This is why option development is so hard.

Practical Application

Here is a systematic process for creative option development. It can be either used individually, or applied as a powerful brainstorm technique with a team:

- Take a new sheet of paper and define your goal as a question: How can I . . . ?
- Write down and number all the possible solutions to this question.
- If the problem is significant, the first 5 to 10 solutions you write down will be fairly easy. They are generated spontaneously by the conscious mind.
- Solutions 10 to 15 will be difficult because they require hard thinking and force you to create new associations. Your initial instinct is to stop thinking and give up. Don't give in to this instinct and continue.
- Solutions 15 to 20 are difficult. However, force yourself to continue until you have written 20 solutions on paper. Oftentimes the breakthrough insights and creative ideas will be found in the last five solutions.
- Pick your best solution. Perform another option-development exercise based on this solution: *How can I . . .* You will be baffled by the brilliance of your own mind.

A scientific training in hard engineering sciences sometimes assumes a single answer to a problem. After all, the world is upside down if 1 plus 1 no longer equals 2. Yet, engineers are also trained to consider multiple options to deal with typical engineering problems. For example, various carmakers apply different technologies to reduce fuel consumption. Therefore, business leaders need to make a clear distinction between digital problems (there is only one answer) and fuzzy problems (there can be multiple answers). Because a business goal is almost always fuzzy and involves all kinds of decision criteria, multiple routes to a solution are possible.

Option development typically happens at two moments in time. The first moment is before you commit to achieving a big goal and start your journey to cross the Valley of Death. This moment is called *exploring options*. The second moment occurs when crossing the Valley of Death, called *portfolio thinking*.

How to Explore Options before Entering the Valley of Death

If you only focus on one route to a solution and put all your eggs in a single basket, you will invite trouble. You burn bridges and shun a plan B. The thinking is that safeguards such as a plan B invite cautious behavior, thus preventing a leader from taking bold steps. The flaw in this approach is that the most successful leaders take bold steps, while at the same time mitigating the downside of risks. If you jump from a plane with a parachute, you have made a bold choice. Adding a spare parachute significantly reduces risk, thus making the jump exciting and relatively safe. If you refrain from adding a spare parachute, you will neither increase the chance of making bold decisions—jumping out of the plane—nor show more persistence when things go pear-shaped. The reason is very simple: You tend to overestimate skill and underestimate luck. A more prudent decision is therefore to create an environment where skills thrive and luck is reduced. You should therefore explore alternatives before entering the Valley of Death.

A strategic plan without options to get there is dangerous. To keep a plane in the air, it is wise to have independent backup systems when things go wrong. This is not always obvious, because many leaders confuse strategic boldness with decision-making boldness. Strategic boldness is a do-or-die strategy. Initially praised by pundits, the bold leader is quickly abandoned when things don't work out well. Think of the carmaker Fisker, which started out with wide approval, yet had to abandon its vision of making electric cars when losses started mounting. Tesla walked the same road and, so far, has made it. This doesn't mean that the Tesla approach to taking risks is a successful one. After all, you may be dealing with survivor bias, devouring the one big story of monumental success, while simply forgetting the many others who didn't make it in our success universe. This is the pitfall of strategic boldness.

Decision boldness, or *triage*, on the other hand, forces an organization to develop options before committing to cross the Valley of Death. As a leader it's important to adopt the mindset of triage when it comes to decision making. Triage is the decision model adopted in field hospitals in war zones. It ensures the survival of the maximum amount of wounded people with a limited medical supply. Triage is a useful model for business leaders, since resources are limited by definition. The idea of triage in business is to never settle for activities with a low-reward or a high-risk profile. After all, it's best to use organizational energy elsewhere. I've seen companies fall in love with extending payment terms to their vendors to save a few dollars, while at the same time losing the plot when it comes to innovation power. This practice is called *myopic optimization*. If the Titanic has been ripped open by an iceberg, don't bother with repairing a leaking sink in the passenger cabin to stop the flooding.

If you find yourself heavy with activities which are both high risk and high reward, it's time to be bold and either develop alternatives with a lesser risk profile or focus on mitigating risk. For example, if you implement a new IT system to logistically serve your customer better, a mitigating strategy is to run both the old and new system in parallel until the new system having proved itself.

Therefore, before you commit to crossing the Valley of Death, ensure that you not only have options to help you achieve success, but also make sure that each option provides a high reward and carries a low risk.

How to Apply Alternatives while Crossing the Valley of Death

If you ask project managers if it's important for their project to be successful, the answer will of course be affirmative. Otherwise, their work is fairly useless and their time can better be used elsewhere. Project managers will therefore do everything in their power to turn an important project into a big success. If you pose the same question to the CEO, the answer would be very different. The CEO looks at all projects and is generally interested only in the aggregate result of the entire basket of initiatives. This is called *portfolio thinking*. In other words, the result of the individual pieces is irrelevant; what counts is the overall result.

For an investor, only the overall result of the entire portfolio matters. In investing, generally speaking, things don't always feel that way. Many investors become itchy when they look at underperforming parts of their portfolios and start making unwise decisions, such as panic selling at the bottom of the market. The same behavior may be true for a CEO: why not cut the cord on the initiatives that are lagging? This decision isn't straightforward though. Are the initiatives lagging because the chances of future performance are very limited, or are the fluctuations in performance due to external circumstances that will likely change? In this case, getting rid of lagging assets would increase risk and decrease performance.

Once they have committed to their goal, leaders therefore need to make a judgment call to apply portfolio thinking correctly while crossing the Valley of Death. The following parameters will help you to make the right decision about which initiatives to continue and which initiatives to kill on your way to achieving your big growth goal.

Predefined Intermediate Milestones

It's never a good idea to start without a good plan. A good plan always contains conditions that need to be met in order to continue to the next phase. For example, when developing a new project, an intermediate predefined milestone could be the first customer sale at a certain moment. If the sale happens, do continue. If the sale fails, quit the project.

Common-Cause Success or Failure

If the success or failure of two different initiatives depend on the same circumstances, you're dealing with a common-cause success or failure. For example, a common-cause failure on safety equipment can be the interruption of power. If both the safety interlocks and the emergency shutdown system depend on the same power supply, you can't rely on the safety performance of the two systems independently. If the power supply fails, they both fail. The same can be true for new initiatives. If the success rate of launching two different products has a common cause, such as the fortune of the same customer for both products, these two products may win or fail at the same time. If you kill one, you may want to kill the other too.

Time Horizon

If you make decisions too quickly, you may destroy a great initiative before it's hatched. If you make them too slowly, you may drag underperformers as anchors on your results. The optimum time horizon depends on your circumstances. In a marketplace with fast and direct feedback, portfolio decisions may happen more often and quickly. This is the principle of *failing fast*. If time horizons are long, such as with reservoir engineering, where oil field development may take a decade or more, it's best to design a broad portfolio with as many eggs as possible, and hang on to this portfolio for a much longer time. Here, you can apply the strengths of accelerated learning.

Why Few Decisions Matter in Overcoming Obstacles

Another interesting phenomenon in stock investing is that over a long period of time, the vast majority of stock market gains occur only on a few days. If you miss these days because you're not invested in the market, you run the risk of missing almost all of the market gains. This is the effect of the *vital few*.

As a business leader, it's not only important to become aware of the *vital few* phenomenon, but it's really helpful to make active use of it. In the end, for business success, only few decisions really matter. Some decisions really count if you want to cross the Valley of Death.

First, do you fall in love with your company, project, and product, or fall in love with your client? One day, I designed a complete, intensive two-day leadership workshop to help a company grow in the next few years. The day before the workshop, a huge reorganization literally changed the complete landscape. If I had fallen in love with my product, not much would have changed in the execution of the workshop—valuable for the customer, for sure, but less applicable because of the changing circumstance. I realized I had to fall in love with the client to help the company further. Overnight, I completely redesigned the workshop. Now it was aimed at giving participants all tools needed to deal with these changes. The outcome was a great success.

Second, do you push your organization to dismiss the mediocre and the obvious, and focus on the bold and breakthrough instead? You will need only a few breakthrough ideas to create an enormous amount of success. On the other hand, you need a lot of small and mediocre ideas to match this achievement. Often, the organizational time and energy spent on executing a few small ideas is not much different from the organizational time and energy spent on a big idea. The question is how do you direct the limited resources of an organization to bold and breakthrough thinking? As you've seen in the previous chapter, a focus on marketing, innovation, and strategy is always a very good use of resources.

Finally, where do you spend your own time as a business leader? Do you anticipate the Valley of Death, push your people to prepare options, explore alternatives, and apply portfolio thinking? Or do you set the vision and hope the organization will get the work done? Your active involvement in driving portfolio thinking and triage is one of the most important leadership activities you can engage in.

Summary and What's Next

This chapter has described a process for crossing the Valley of Death. This process builds on your strengths as engineers. Reality-based thinking ensures that you expect and prepare for big obstacles on your way to achieving your goals. Applying triage before crossing the Valley of Death ensures that you select the options with the highest up side and the lowest down side. While crossing the Valley of Death, you can use accelerated learning to actively look for feedback on your progress and apply portfolio thinking to maximize your chances of success.

Now that you have seen several strategies that build on engineering strengths to cross the Valley of Death, the following chapter will focus on the next piece of the goal-achieving puzzle: How does your behavior as a leader influence your ability to achieve big growth goals?

External Perspective

Interview of Marcel Berkhout, CFO, MeDirect Bank

What Has Been the Most Fascinating Aspect of Business Leadership for You?
We are a young bank in a dynamic environment. Our bank is showing business leadership through our innovative client approach. It's amazing how much we can achieve with our dedicated team of great professionals, by simply putting all our energy and focus on those parts of the financial industry where we are at our best.

Our leadership can also be evidenced in our new ways of working. As CFO of the bank, I'm heading our financial reporting and balance sheet management. I work out of Brussels. Yet, a large part of my team is located in Malta and London. We work together intensively with, for example, lots of conference calls and other forms of interaction. Our *modus operandi* is fascinating but can be quite demanding.

What Are Some of the Most Important Skills and Behaviors for Business Leaders with an Engineering Background to Improve their Effectiveness?
As engineers, we are trained to be precise with numbers. Yet, when taking a decision, a good feeling for the order of magnitude of a number and understanding second-order effects of the decision are equally important.

Let me make this more concrete through two examples. The engineer at a refinery who considers changing the temperature in a distillation column, needs to understand the materiality of the change and the effects further downstream in the process. Similarly, at a bank, when we decide about our treasury bond portfolio, it is not only a matter of assessing risk and return, but also assessing the effect on the bank's solvency and liquidity ratios. Having an engineering background helps.

Engineers need to be careful to embrace the idea that developing leadership skills can only be achieved through formal "management" skills trainings. In my view, it's important to remain authentic, otherwise you lose credibility. The fastest way to grow as a leader is by leading, adjusting your behavior based on feedback from the people around you, and always enjoying what you are doing.

What Is Your Approach to Learning and Improving as a Business Leader Yourself?

With experience, you also gain perspective. It's a sign of maturity to admit mistakes. This has enabled me to improve my own judgment. Also, the biggest setbacks have been the biggest learning opportunities for me.

What I have found is that often informal conversations with leaders and professionals from different fields provide great new ideas. I want to reserve more time for this kind of opportunity to learn and grow.

CHAPTER 5

Effective Leadership Behaviors

Which behaviors will help you cross the Valley of Death, how can you build these behaviors for yourself, and how can you change the behaviors of others?

Why Effective Leadership Behaviors Matter

On August 15, 1977, something remarkable happened. A strong radio signal was received by Ohio State University's Big Ear radio telescope. Its source? The constellation Sagittarius. It had all the characteristics of extraterrestrial origin. Astronomer Jerry Ehman looked at the result and wrote the comment *Wow!* on the computer printout. Until this very day, the Wow! event remains unexplained, yet it carries a valuable lesson. In a world full of noise, a distinct signal has power to stand apart like a tall giraffe surrounded by tiny field mice. The ability for a leader to help an organization focus on behaviors that separate noise from signal is a key skill for achieving big goals. It is the ability to see what others, such as the competition, can't. In order to do this, you have two options: Either *boost signal* or *decrease noise*.

How to Boost Signal

How do you detect leaks in gas pipelines that are hundreds of miles long? Some decades ago, a group of perceptive oil engineers noticed something interesting. Gas leaks were often accompanied by groups of turkey vultures circling above. What they found was that ethyl mercaptan, the smelly stuff added to natural gas, resembled odor coming from decaying bodies, thus attracting vultures. The engineers had the presence of mind to recognize a key piece of data and put this into action. In the oil industry, vulture-watching has become common practice to find gas leaks in pipelines.

What can we learn from this analogy? A proven leadership behavior to recognize and boost signal, and focus on what really matters is to look at your organization and ask yourself, "What shouldn't work, but is working anyway?" For example, while studying the business of professional speaking, I noticed that the top earners appeared to be fairly weak in sales. Their language was timid, proposals were mediocre, and closing techniques were nonexistent most of the time. Yet, many were in the top 10 percent of income earners. I was puzzled. How was this even possible? What struck me was they invariably did one thing totally differently from what everyone else did. They doggedly followed up every speaking engagement with the question, "Which people do you know, who could use my help?" And then, they deliberately collected the names and persistently followed up. They had built a smooth and effective referral engine that became the driver of their success.

How to Decrease Noise

A client of mine once got stuck trying to improve safety performance. Whenever an incident occurred, it was investigated and invariably resulted in adding additional safety rules. It became a ritual, full of symbolic actions, yet signifying little. In time, his safety rule book grew until only specialists could make sense of the patchwork of rules. And yet, the safety performance of my client's team didn't improve. Courageously, he and his team decided to do something different. In their communication, they didn't use the safety rulebook, but only focused on 10 critical safety rules and explained, coached, and enforced these rules with vigor. This concrete step happened to be the breakthrough to decrease noise and improve safety performance.

To make change stick, it's important to focus on behaviors that cut out noise in your own environment first. Ask yourself what is really needed to make a bold next step. Then solicit the ideas and help from experts in the field, who are practitioners with a track record of outstanding results.

Often the hardest part for a leader is to ignore everyone else. The rock star Alice Cooper once told a story to drive this point home.

If you're listening to a rock star in order to get your information on who to vote for, you're a bigger moron than they are. Why are we rock stars? Because we're morons. We sleep all day, we play music at night and very rarely do we sit around reading the *Washington Journal*.

There is a lot of wisdom in these words. To get a water leak fixed, listen carefully to your plumber. Ignore him though when it comes to advice about your nutritional needs.

How to Influence Behaviors with the Principles of *Poka Yoke*

The two examples of boosting signal and decreasing noise show that by changing their own behaviors to focus on what really matters, a business leader is able to help an organization to achieve big goals. How can business leaders change their own behaviors (and the behaviors of others) to consistently focus on what really matters? Here you can apply your engineering strength by designing a process based on the principles of *poka yoke*. Poka yoke is a Japanese term that refers to any mechanism to help avoid mistakes. Its purpose is to eliminate deviations by preventing, correcting, or drawing attention to human errors as they occur. For example, the key to my car can be removed only when its transmission is fixed in park (P). This poka yoke mechanism ensures that the distracted me never forgets to put the car in park before taking out the key.

The approach of poka yoke gives a simple framework to influence behaviors and massively improve your ability to cross the Valley of Death. Two key elements of a poka yoke device are simplicity and standardization. Think of an electricity plug. It's a simple device (two or more metal prongs that fit into holes of the same depth) that has a uniform design (same plugs and same size, depending on geographical area). What if you could design a behavioral poka yoke based on the same two characteristics: simplicity and standardization?

Simplicity: In Tolkien's epic story *The Lord of the Rings*, there were 19 rings of power in the fantasy world of Middle Earth. Yet there was only One Ring designed to rule them all. Organizations with a lot of strategic goals generally create a lot of noise and run the risk of watering down their execution power. Which one goal, if you would achieve it right here and right now, would have the biggest impact on your business? For leaders, simplicity often means to focus on this one goal and making every other goal support it.

Standardization: In hindsight, when Columbus set sail to explore the New World, he didn't know where he was going. Once he arrived in the Americas, he didn't know where he was, and when he returned to Spain, he didn't know where he had been. The story of Columbus is a fitting metaphor for the way many organizations drift through life. They have vague ideas of where they want to go. They are confused of where they are. And they're clueless about what happened to them in the past. This quagmire is called the *Columbus confusion*. As we have seen in Chapter 1, clarity about cross-functional goals is essential to improving execution power. If you're unclear in this area, things can go horribly wrong.

Recently, leaders in the purchasing department of a big corporate client of mine decided to improve cash flow by extending payment terms to its suppliers. An edict was sent to all suppliers with the message that as of now, the new payment terms would be enforced. Little did they realize that many of their suppliers were also clients for other parts of the business. To their dismay they found that these clients promptly returned the favor by adopting the same unfavorable payment terms in their businesses as well. This typical case of cross-functional myopia is caused by a lack of goal standardization and identical goal design.

To ensure identical cross-functional design of corporate goals, you must realize that you will not see how to do it until you see yourself doing it. In other words, a corporate goal becomes meaningful only when it is connected to behaviors. For example, a key behavior to grow the top line of any company is to ensure that every single executive brings in business. By connecting a corporate goal (top-line growth) to a simple, standard behavior that applies to all executives (every single executive is accountable to see prospects and clients), cross-functional alignment is ensured. This will significantly improve the goal-achieving power of your organization as well.

How to Lead Effectively with Behavioral Distinctions

The culture of an organization is driven by mindsets that govern actions. As described earlier, a new goal requires building a new culture. Three important elements of a culture are language, stories, and metaphors. For example, one of my clients is famous for a culture that is able to quickly focus on the heart of the matter by engaging in frank, and sometimes uncomfortable, conversations. They use the metaphor of *putting the dead rat on the table* to start critical conversations.

To change the culture of an organization to support the new goals quickly, you need to actively bring in language, stories, and metaphors that support your objectives. The best way to boost signal and reduce noise around language, stories, and metaphors is to start working with *behavioral distinctions*. A behavioral distinction creates a clear boundary between what is and what is not. A powerful behavioral distinction, however, does not make the difference between good and bad behavior, but instead draws the line between just getting by and real acceleration. Take for instance the behavioral bromide *result-driven*. Naturally, no organization likes to be known as a slacker, so result-driven may actually apply to every organization in our known universe (and beyond if you are into that kind of thing). The distinction between result-driven and its opposite—not result-driven—is therefore not a very good distinction. The distinction between result-driven and process-driven, on the other hand, is much better.

A good distinction is wrapped in simple language and at the same time provides a standard interpretation. Working with good distinctions therefore acts as a poka yoke for building new mindsets. Effective leadership requires both awareness and application of outstanding distinctions. Reality-based thinking plays a leading role for leaders with an engineering background. It's by understanding and acknowledging reality that true distinctions can be addressed. Here are 12 distinctions that will raise the bar and rapidly take you to the next level of performance.

Playing to Win versus Playing Not to Lose

Imagine you like to watch soccer. One day, as you flip through channels you stumble upon a game with two unfamiliar teams. You decide to keep on watching and notice something interesting. One team is clearly *playing to win* and the other team is playing not to lose. The team *playing not to lose* is temporizing, fearful, and focused on stalling progress. The team playing to win is eager, obsessed with using time as best as possible, and moving forward. If you are a neutral observer, you will probably start to root for the team focused on winning.

Leaders of organizations focused on winning instead of not losing:

- Are willing to try new things in order to abandon the old ways and even make themselves obsolete. Philip Morris, the tobacco company, is explicitly working to decrease tobacco use and has a clear business objective to make itself obsolete in the business area of selling tobacco. This goal is driven by a belief that there is no future in tobacco, and thus it's best to create a new future themselves.
- Focus on new opportunities and ignore lobbying efforts to influence new legalization to create a competitive edge. For example, if you take a close look at the recent European *Reach*-directive to monitor and control any adverse effects of new and existing chemicals, you may conclude it has been specifically designed to lock out small competitors and support big companies able to carry the burden of adhering to vast and cumbersome legislation. Critics have argued that if Reach had been in place 30 years ago, we may never have benefited from many new chemicals and materials we're currently taking for granted.
- View risk as part of the price of doing business and actually manage it in a portfolio style. In other words, being comfortable with and even expecting failure of several initiatives to achieve your goals, while having other opportunities up and running at the same time, may lead to great results.

Executive Question

Where do you reward behaviors in your organization, focused on playing to win, acting boldly, and courageously moving ahead into the unknown?

Owner versus Victim

Ownership is about the decision to continue to expand skill and talent to reach your goals. *Victimhood* means blaming circumstances and hoping that luck will move you to your most important goals. There is no power in victimhood. If results are based on luck, there is not much you can do and improvement is not controllable. The drive to expand ownership to achieve personal and organizational goals is a key behavior for any leader.

While working with a somewhat dysfunctional management team, I started the session with a list of past successes and miserable failures. Naturally, the successes were attributed to skill, while most failures were caused by dire circumstances and bad luck. After I explained the concept of owner versus victim, we went through the list of failures again. We asked ourselves the question: *If we had shown more ownership, could the result have been different?* With every bullet point, the answer was affirmative.

For leaders with an engineering background, taking full ownership is key to massively improving the goal-achieving power of your organization. It's especially helpful to take full control of the three strengths that you bring as a leader to start taking back and expanding ownership: reality-based thinking, process design, and accelerated learning.

Executive Question

What is the biggest issue your business is facing right now? How can you apply your three engineering strengths to act more like an owner and less like a victim to deal with this issue?

Student versus Follower

Have you ever gone back in your mind a decade or so? If so, you may probably have noticed some interesting things.

First, the things that were important at that time are probably no longer on your radar. Did you really stress out over that project? Were these the most important business problems at that time? It shows that the world is not only changing, but you adapt and change with it. Yet, these changes are so natural and often gradual that you may not notice you have changed as well.

This leads to the second observation: Many core beliefs, assumptions, and truisms no longer ring true. We no longer follow a certain leadership philosophy. We might even consider our past cherished beliefs about business, leadership, and management somewhat naive. This healthy development is driven by curiosity. However, we may also realize along the way that we have exchanged a healthy curiosity for a set of dogmatic beliefs as a leader. In some areas, we may have moved from being a *student* to becoming a *follower*.

Though looking back will usually put this transformation into sharp perspective, it's often very difficult to see this phenomenon in the here and now. As a leader, you run the risk of exchanging curiosity for certainty. It's a comfortable position, yet it can be deadly for judgment.

Executive Question

Where do you need to force yourself and your organization to behave like a student, instead of a follower? Where do you need to step out of dogmatic thinking and become more curious instead?

Substance versus Symbolism

A symbolic action gives a message yet accomplishes little. Take the CEO who travels with his private jet yet lectures the world about energy reduction. Or politicians who make the rules for others and incorporate exceptions for themselves. This phenomenon is called *moral licensing*. By doing good deeds in one area, you allow yourself to slip in others.

In order to move from *symbolism* to *substance*, it's best to consciously start role-modeling the behaviors you would like to see in your people. If you think that a certain behavior is important, you'd better model this behavior yourself, consistently at every occasion.

A big oil firm has taken this approach to heart. They are committed to safety from the top down. Whenever business leaders in this company want to invest a significant amount of money, they're invited to have an audience with the Board at headquarters. The first question from the

Board is invariably: "How's your safety performance?" If they don't like the answer, the leaders will be sent away without even having the opportunity to discuss their proposal. The senior leadership of this company is convinced that you can't have a successful investment unless your safety performance is excellent. They don't engage in symbolism. They focus on substance instead.

Executive Question

Where do you need to raise the bar as a leader to stop symbolism and start to provide substance by consciously role-modeling the behaviors you would like to see on a consistent basis.

Committed versus Involved

The classic observation is when you have eggs with bacon for breakfast, the chicken is involved and the pig is committed. This is also true for business. When you're *committed* to an initiative, you will have skin in the game. If it fails, you will fail. However, if you're *involved*, the initiative may fail, yet you won't feel the consequences.

Being committed entails an enormous sense of urgency. This is one of the things you need in order to cross the Valley of Death and achieve big goals. There are some things you can do to ensure commitment as a leader.

First, reward the overall result of the organization. Make clear that no additional bonuses are forthcoming unless the most important business goals have been achieved. For example, when I was involved in improving the safety performance of a company by changing mindsets and behaviors, safety performance became the multiplier for all bonuses. All of a sudden, everyone realized that by changing their own behaviors, they had a part to play in safety.

Next, ensure the link between involvement and enlightened self-interest. People change for a few reasons. One is compliance: You will get fired if you don't adhere to the change. Another is peer pressure: Everyone else is doing it, so it's helpful for you to do it as well. And then there's enlightened self-interest: If we're successful as a company, how will it help your personal goals? Self-interest is the strongest driver for lasting change.

When I was helping a leadership team adopt the behaviors of ownership of the goals of this team, they quickly came on board when they realized that the behaviors we were working on would help the next level teams they were leading themselves as well.

Executive Question

Is your entire organization committed to, or only involved in, its most important goal? Which behavior can you show as a leader to increase commitment?

Serving versus Pleasing

On January 27, 1986, Thiokol engineers and managers discussed the weather conditions surrounding the upcoming launch of the Space Shuttle Challenger with their counterparts from NASA. The weather was very cold and one of the design engineers, Roger Boisjoly, pointed out the negative impact of low temperatures on the resilience of the rubber O-rings that sealed the fuel rocket joints. He recommended a launch postponement. His bosses refused to bring that recommendation to NASA leadership. As a result, on January 28, the Challenger exploded, only 73 seconds after launch, caused by a failed O-ring.

Sugarcoating difficult messages in order to keep the peace and avoid confrontation might make people happy in the short run, but it's devastating for long-term success. *Pleasing* typically happens during interaction with customers. After all, you want to make our customers happy. Yet by playing *yes man* to your customers, you may miss an opportunity to really *serve* them.

Executive Question

In what areas of your business are you pleasing when you should instead be serving?

Results versus Process

The danger of a good process is that it becomes its own objective. This is the definition of bureaucracy: the triumph of *process* over *results*. In bigger companies, processes are core to any operation. Without processes, chaos would reign. Yet, if taken to the extreme, adherence to processes to achieve a goal becomes more important than the goal itself.

When I once ran an engineering department, we had a process describing in detail how to do projects. It was very systematic, transparent, and had several stakeholders accountable for each of the steps. We had one problem though. Projects were slow, expensive, and risky. Overruns were happening more than 80 percent of the time. The entire process was simply not effective. The problem was that many improvement efforts in the past were focused on optimizing parts of the process, yet none focused on the overall results. We finally got unstuck by asking a simple question: What are we trying to achieve here anyway?

Since process design is a strength of engineers, the risk is they fall in love with a process, instead of falling in love with results. A good leader, therefore, makes the distinction between a process and a result to ensure the right things get done.

Executive Question

Where has your organization fallen in love with processes and lost sight of the overall result?

Add Value versus Taking Up Space

Do you speak up to be heard and *take up space*, or do you speak up to *add value*? If you feel you need to dominate a discussion, you simply add to the noise in order to stake your territory.

I often see this in client presentations. Most of the slides are about the company, its history, values, etc. Very few slides are about how to improve the client's condition.

Practical Application

Here is a neat little trick to evaluate if you are adding value or just taking up space in client conversations. Next time you give a presentation to a client, write *me* or *you* on every single slide. A *you* slide adds value to the client, while a *me* slide simply takes up space. Redo the presentation to ensure that less than 10 percent of your presentation contains *me* slides

Executive Question

Where can you improve your key presentations, take less space, and focus more on adding value to your customers?

Speaking with Clarity versus Speaking in Code

Have you ever noticed how language drives discussion? The hallways of business are ripe with profound words that have lost any meaning. Think of the ubiquitous buzzwords "win–win," "agile," or "sustainable." The improper use of coded language gives rise to many misunderstandings. You saw earlier that clarity is the first step in goal achieving. It's important for leaders to also apply clarity to their use of language.

Clarity in language starts by setting the standards. *This is what I expect from you* is a good start for conversations with your employees.

Another best practice applies to teams. It helps to discuss together the behaviors necessary to achieve top performance. In my strategy work, this conversation usually ends with a list entitled: *We are at our best when . . .* Typical elements in this list may be:

- We agree with what is going on if we remain silent.
- We make decisions as a team based on the best available information and review the decisions only when new information pops up.
- We proactively discuss when the initiative is in jeopardy.
- We discuss internally and speak with one voice externally.
- We are respectfully nice to each other.
- We celebrate success and use mistakes as learning opportunities.

Executive Question

What behaviors bring out the best in your team members, and how can you speak with clarity to make these behaviors explicit?

Honoring Your Word versus Giving Your Word

Saying yes is easy. Doing what you say you'll do is much harder. Your subconscious brain remembers every commitment you make to others, and especially every commitment you make to yourself. The problem is that your subconscious can't discern importance, space, or time. In other words, if you give your word to paint the bedroom, some part of your brain thinks you should be painting the bedroom right now, all the time.

This example illustrates that giving your word to others and especially giving your word to yourself is of utmost importance for your leadership success. You can give your word only when you know everything you've committed to. Thus, saying yes or no to new initiatives is impossible until you have a complete overview of all your other commitments.

If you've made a commitment that, because of circumstances outside your control that you can't keep, you need to renegotiate. Effective leaders are very keen on honoring their word, and go out of their way to make a new agreement when it becomes clear they cannot keep the commitment.

Executive Question

If agreements are ignored often in your organization, which standards do you set for honoring your word as a leader?

Evidence versus Anecdotes

Reality-based thinking is always based on evidence: a set of verifiable facts that provide the best effort to paint a complete picture of the issue at hand. While building the complete picture, one of the typical pitfalls is to confuse *anecdotes* with *evidence*. Anecdotes are snippets of data. For example, one customer complaining that things are not working is an anecdote. Many customers complaining about the same thing becomes evidence. This concept isn't limited to business, but is becoming more and more important in academia as well. Some estimates reveal that experiments from more than 50 percent of all peer-reviewed articles in behavioral psychology can't be replicated. What is presented as data, is actually anecdotal evidence.

Effective leadership is therefore about pressing for evidence and ignoring data that is purely anecdotal.

Executive Question

When should you be more curious, rely less on anecdotes, and ask, "Where's the evidence for that?"

Building a Legacy versus Leaving a Trail

The size of your funeral will be determined by the weather. For many, this realization is both disheartening and sobering. Our natural tendency is to think we matter, which explains why the words *why*, *meaning*, and *legacy* have recently become an important part of the vocabulary of business leaders. Often when leaders leave, their signature DNA leaves the organization as well. Think of Allied Signal, which quickly lost its execution prowess when legendary CEO Larry Bossidy retired. Distinctions not only create behaviors necessary to achieve big goals, but they also ensure that your legacy remains when you are gone. The reason is that as a leader, the minimum effective behavior you show yourself, is the maximum effective behavior you can expect from others. By consistently role-modeling good behaviors, you are therefore able to change the behaviors of others. This is the difference between *leaving a trail* and *building a legacy*.

Executive Question

Which legacy do you want to leave behind as a business leader?

Table 5.1 gives an overview of all 12 behavioral distinctions and how to apply these distinctions as a leader to change an organizational culture.

Table 5.1 The impact of behavioral distinctions on an organizational culture

Behavioral distinction	Impact on organizational culture
Playing to win versus playing not to lose	Improve innovation
Owner versus victim	Improve ownership and pro-activity
Student versus follower	Improve external orientation and customer intimacy
Substance versus symbolism	Improve learning
Committed versus involved	Improve strategic alignment
Serving versus pleasing	Improve customer intimacy and trust

(continued)

Table 5.1 (continued)

Behavioral distinction	Impact on organizational culture
Results versus process	Improve customer value
Add value versus taking up space	Improve innovation and customer intimacy
Speaking straight versus speaking in code	Improve clarity and alignment
Honoring your word versus giving your word	Improve execution power
Evidence versus anecdotes	Improve decision making
Leaving a trail versus building a legacy	Improve long term perspective

Summary and What's Next

The leadership behaviors of focusing on boosting signal and reducing noise give you a chance to consistently build a culture that supports your ambitious growth goals. While you can't influence the weather at your funeral, you can use the poka yoke approach to focus on simplicity and standardization to influence mindsets and behaviors. By using behavioral distinctions, you apply simplicity and standardization to shape the right language, stories, and metaphors. These will not only help you achieve your current goals, but will build a legacy and influence your organization far into the future.

Part III of this book covered the three elements of focus: engineering strengths, overcoming obstacles, and leadership behaviors. Even exceptionally skilled and talented business leaders will play a lousy business game if they are in the dark and unable to focus. Now, it's time to move to Part IV: execution. The next chapter will explain how your ability to strategically quit can massively improve your execution power.

External Perspective

Interview of Jian, Chairman of the Board of Fujian Newland EnTech Co. Ltd.

What Are Some of the Most Important Skills for Business Leaders with an Engineering Background to Improve their Effectiveness?
The most important skills for a business leader are still the same as those required for the quality of a normal leader. Typical examples

(continued)

are the power of execution, enthusiasm of working, the capabilities of organization, interpersonal skills, etc. With an engineering background, a big advantage for a business leader is that he knows very well the key part of what the company relies on: products.

Which Trends Do You See that May Be Relevant for Leaders with an Engineering Background to Have a Bigger Impact in the Future?

Currently, there are many trends that will change greatly our style of living, such as Internet systems, portable communication equipment, artificial intelligence, robots, automatics, and clean energy (all of non-fossil energies).

What Is Your Approach to Learning and Improving as a Business Leader Yourself?

There are several important things that change you from an engineer to a leader. First, you should have plentiful experience of social contact, interpersonal, and inter-natural, when you grow up. This means not only staying at home and sitting in front of the computer. Next, you should read relevant books by yourself. Furthermore, use your eyes, your ears, and your head to learn carefully from any good quality of others surrounding you in daily life. Finally, when going to college, take lessons for a system to study.

PART IV

If You Think You're in Control, You're Not Going Fast Enough

CHAPTER 6

Strategic Quitting

How do you find the time, money, and energy to continue moving toward your goals?

Why Strategic Quitting Matters

When I was a young boy, I was totally in love with playing chess. I was also clumsy, skinny, and somewhat pale. My parents decided that something needed to be done, so they took me to the doctor. The doctor was quick in her diagnosis that I needed to be outside in the sunshine. My father promptly took me to a playground and pointed at the monkey bar: a horizontal set of bars hanging in the air. Children were having fun moving from bar to bar. My father lifted me up and I was hanging there with white knuckles and stiff as a board. After a few seconds my father advised that if I wanted to move ahead, I had to let go in order to reach out. I was an obedient boy, thus I let go. Unfortunately, I let go with both hands, so half an hour later I was back in the doctor's office with a sprained ankle. The doctor, helpful as always, told me next time I was dangling in the air, I had to let go strategically. This seems to be good advice for businesses as well. If you want to cross the Valley of Death and move toward your goals, you have to quit existing activities in order to engage in new activities. This is called *strategic quitting*.

The ability to let go of existing activities in order to do new and better ones is key for business success. For example, when Jack Welch became CEO of General Electric (GE) in the 1980s, he applied strategic quitting vigorously. GE was a conglomerate of many businesses. He decided that if a business could not be number one or number two in the marketplace, GE would discontinue this business in its portfolio. Doing so would free up time, energy, and leadership focus to make strong businesses even stronger. His philosophy was if you're not competitive, simply don't compete. This strategy proved to be the basis of one of the most successful business turnarounds of the past century.

Strategic quitting is not limited to businesses, but can be applied to individuals as well. It's probably surprising to many people that Albert Einstein was relatively weak in mathematics. Thus, while he developed the theory of relativity, he had an advanced team of very smart mathematicians work out all the details. He let go of the ambition to become excellent at mathematics to focus on his true strength of physics.

Why Strategic Quitting Is Effective

Many great goals are abandoned because of procrastination while crossing the Valley of Death. We have covered several ideas to overcome procrastination, such as portfolio thinking, triage, and focus on the vital few. Strategic quitting provides another tool to help achieve big goals. This tool acts on a very deep emotional level. Chapter 4 introduced the tug-of-war between the lizard brain and neocortex. Unstoppable goal achievers know another secret of the lizard brain: Its favorite activity is to quit. For example, imagine you make a new year's resolution to become serious about your health and fitness. Thus, you buy a trendy workout outfit, load your iPhone with energizing music, and obtain a fitness center membership. Typically, after a few workout days, you start to reduce the amount of exercise and even skip sessions. Before long, you may quit it altogether. This pattern is due to sabotage from your lizard brain. It slowly convinces you that it's no use and you should quit now to get back to your general comfort zone. It wins when you finally quit.

An interesting way to use this lizard brain tendency while you are crossing the Valley of Death is to simply give in and give it other things to quit. Yet, make sure these things are not important to achieve your goals. Metaphorically speaking, you are feeding the crocodile—the hungry lizard—to ensure it stays quiet and let you finish your work. Practically speaking, a focus on strategic quitting will significantly increase your chances of crossing the Valley of Death. Yet, this approach is counterintuitive to how organizations usually work, which entails a somewhat different script:

- A new, big initiative/strategy/goal is dreamed up, usually at headquarters.
- Key executives are rallied to communicate the big thing throughout the organization.
- With various levels of enthusiasm, employees start to focus on making the big thing work. This, however, is usually on top of their existing workload, which often causes them to overstretch and unfortunately creates additional stress.
- The additional stress has a negative impact on operational performance and productivity. Instead of exploring new frontiers, the employees in the organization have to play catch-up.
- Naturally, seeing the numbers slide, leaders challenge their people to work harder. They don't realize that *doing more* is not the answer to *too much to do*.
- When an organization reaches breaking point, senior executives are forced to embrace triage: something needs to be done. The initiative is either quietly abandoned, or tough decisions are made, usually involving quitting stuff.
- Only after freeing up energy and time by strategically quitting activities, is progress finally made on the new big thing.

The question, therefore, is not *if* you will adopt strategic quitting. The question is *when* you will adopt strategic quitting. Your role as a leader is therefore to think big and at the same time have the courage to drive strategic quitting as a core activity in your organization.

How to Apply Strategic Quitting to Achieve Strategic Goals

Your most important growth goals are usually part of a corporate strategic plan. The chance of a new strategy succeeding depends on including strategic quitting as a core part of this plan. Signals that this part is missing are:

- Limited or no written statements in the strategy on what exactly will be abandoned in order to make the new strategy work.
- Mention of vague and unspecified productivity improvements to release time and energy to make the new strategy work.

- Timid statements about studying possible future business decisions regarding quitting activities.
- Fluffy and uncommitted language, such as *"Based on progress, we will evaluate how to proceed with other initiatives."*

Your role as a leader is to flesh out in detail the strategic quitting part of any goal, strategy, or initiative before you commit the organization to the Valley of Death. One of the most powerful tools to do so is *zero-based thinking*. This is how zero-based thinking works: If you want to find areas where you can apply the concept of strategic quitting, look at your business as a consultant and ask yourself, "Knowing what I know right now, which activities would I not have started if I could do it all over again?" This is a powerful question, because many actions were started to meet a need or solve a problem. Yet, the environment has changed and these actions may no longer serve the need or solve the problem. The activities, however, have become an organizational habit and people tend to only become aware of their habits when they consciously think about them. Thus, quitting a habit is a deliberate and conscious activity that doesn't come naturally to any organization. This phenomenon is called the *momentum fallacy*. Once an object or activity is in motion, it takes a lot of effort to stop it. This truth explains why the best predictor of what you will be doing 5 minutes from now is what you are doing at this moment.

We see examples of the momentum fallacy everywhere. Take for example the Mini car. When the Mini was developed in the 1950s, an important design consideration was low cost. Thus, to paint the car, the chassis would be held in the air by a pole that protruded from the back to the front of the car. This pole caused a hole in the middle of the dashboard. The design engineers were classical pragmatists and decided to use this hole to fit the instrument cluster. Thus, the iconic design feature of having an instrument cluster, not in front of the driver, but in between the driver and passenger, was born. Though this setup was arguably inferior to an instrument cluster placed in front of the driver, it has been mindlessly copied in many other automobiles, despite the fact that modern technologies have rendered the pole-painting technique obsolete. This example shows that behaviors and activities will last until long after the reason for having them to begin with has disappeared. Killing activities is hard, and is why challenging assumptions with reality-based thinking is so important to make strategic quitting work.

Practical Application

Zero-based thinking helps you apply reality-based thinking and identify activities to quit. A zero-based thinking exercise, called *Lights on, now what?*, has the following setup:

- Imagine you just bought the company you are currently working for. You're part of the new management team and this is your first day in the office. You switch on the lights, and ask yourself: Now what?
- Imagine you have no history and not a single constraint, and then ask yourself the following:
    - Which activities would I start immediately?
    - Which activities would I stop immediately?
    - Which activities would I do more of?
    - Which activities would I do less of?
- Define the most important activities that help you cross the Valley of Death and start taking action.

How to Apply Strategic Quitting in Your Organization

Time, money, and energy in any organization are by definition limited. As a business leader, it's therefore important to constantly look for opportunities to free up time, money, and energy. Thus, you need to understand where to apply strategic quitting in order to have the biggest impact. To understand how, it's important to fully understand the 80/20 rule. This rule was originally coined by the Italian statistician Vilfredo Pareto, who discovered that 80 percent of the land in Italy was owned by 20 percent of the people. This observation expanded to other areas of economic life as well and was called the 80/20 rule. Upon further study, it became clear the 80/20 rule was not limited to human endeavors, but extended to other fields as well. For example, 80 percent of the lion cubs born in nature come from 20 percent of the lion males. The 80/20 rule tells you that nature is unbalanced. It also means that the results of your efforts are unpredictable, and the relationship between input and output is not linear. The good news is you can make use of this law to get extraordinary results with the least amount of effort.

There are certain areas where the benefits of strategic quitting with the 80/20 rule in mind may have a huge impact on any business.

Training

Approximately $130 billion is spent on training every year in the United States. The idea is that training is an essential component for productivity growth. Yet, measurement of training effectiveness is rather uncommon. When was the last time the return on investment of an actual training was calculated? Furthermore, most training evaluations tend to focus on smile sheets and happiness of the participants, which is hardly a proper yardstick. It's much better to measure the impact of the participant's performance by simply asking his or her boss. An effective training is therefore focused on improving performance rather than potential. From a leadership point of view, the difference is between actual immediate application and future possible application. If I train my people to improve the sales conversion of proposals, I'll improve business quickly. If I train my people to design a launch strategy for some future breakthrough product, I may have to wait a long time to see any benefits.

Executive Question

Before committing to a training program, ask yourself: Will the participants be able to apply the new skills to accelerate achievement of the most important growth goals of the business? If the answer is no, the training is a good candidate for strategic quitting.

Performance Reviews

A performance review is only effective when the feedback is immediate, so people can adjust quickly and improve. In many organizations the ritual of the performance review happens every year. This is odd. First of all, you've seen how frequency, size, and speed of feedback drives accelerated learning. Thus, a year is a very long period between feedback. Any new issues should have been brought up way before any lasting damage occurs. Second, performance reviews typically focus on the weaknesses, or in corporate jargon: development areas. As argued before, it's much easier to build on strengths than try to compensate weaknesses.

Executive Question

How would you apply strategic quitting regarding the performance review system to improve the speed and quality of feedback in your organization?

Innovation

The vast majority of your innovation initiatives will fail. That's the nature of doing things differently. Effective leadership should focus on spending the least amount of resources on the initiatives that are doomed to fail anyway.

Typical signs that an innovation is doomed to fail are:

- Has it been done before? If not, what makes the organization qualified to make it happen this time?
- Do we see a similar approach or application elsewhere in a different industry or marketplace? For example, some approaches to safety systems of nuclear plants can easily be used as input for the design of self-driving cars. Don't reinvent the wheel if you can get a proven blueprint somewhere else.
- Can you reduce the downside while increasing the upside? If the downside of failure is huge, why would you want to put your eggs in this particular basket? If the upside is small (a better mousetrap), you could ask the same question.

Customers

Strategic quitting is especially relevant when it comes to customers. If you look at your client list, you will typically notice that 80 percent of your revenue and/or margin will come from only 20 percent of your customers. The opposite is also true: 80 percent of your headaches will come from 20 percent of your customers as well. The interesting thing is that these two sets of customers are very different.

Practical Application

A good way to grow a business and get better customers is to go through your customer list and fire the bottom 20 percent of your customers every year. This exercise will free up time, energy, and money to find better customers, or improve your service to your existing customers. If this sounds too radical, don't fire your bottom customers, but simply introduce them to your competition.

Cost Reduction

Cost reduction acts as an advanced form of organizational hygiene. It keeps an organization on its toes and ensures a smooth operation by taking out weed so the garden can bloom. However, you can go too far in cost cutting. A constant obsession with cutting costs will typically lead to more organizational time and energy focused on squeezing the last dollar out of your operation. The problem here is twofold. First of all, the relative impact of additional cost savings on your bottom line is limited. If the first 5 percent of cost reduction costs a certain amount of energy, the second 5 percent will cost exponentially more. This is the reverse 80/20 rule in action: After quitting the easy stuff that yields the bulk of savings, you will have to move to the hard stuff, which will hardly improve your bottom line. Since energy is a limited resource, cost cutting cuts directly into more important initiatives like innovation, marketing, or strategy. No organization has ever overcome huge obstacles by simply cutting cost, and the message you send to your organization is that cost cutting is the default solution to improvement. Nothing can be further from the truth. Don't confuse organizational hygiene with growing the top line of your organization.

Executive Question

If it's necessary to focus on cost reduction, ask yourself where can you use 20 percent of the effort to quickly meet 80 percent of the cost-saving objectives?

Meetings

The corporate joke is that if you're bored, call a meeting. Many organizational cultures are choked by meetings deemed necessary to keep an organization running. To streamline your meetings, it's important to realize that meetings have only three purposes: decision making, brainstorming, or driving a project. Virtually all other meetings can be replaced by a more efficient method of information exchange, such as email. One of the most powerful things you can do as a leader is evaluate your meetings on whether they can be cancelled or made more effective.

Practical Application

To make meetings more effective, make use of Parkinson's law, which says that a meeting expands to fill its scheduled time. If you have scheduled an hour, you will probably meet for an hour, even if the key decision was made after 10 minutes. A simple way of overcoming Parkinson's law is to schedule all meetings in half the time. You will see that the meetings not only become much shorter, but the quality will improve as well.

Reporting

Sometimes the major product of any given business is to produce paper driven by huge reporting efforts. A limited amount of time is spent analyzing reports and taking necessary actions. Reporting is therefore typically an area that should be viewed with a keen strategic quitting eye.

Many reports were historically triggered by a need. Because the world has changed, the question is whether reporting still fills this need. There is no such thing as a sunshine clause in reporting. Once a report is produced, it typically continues to be produced.

Practical Application

An interesting idea to fight reporting clutter is, compile a report but don't send it out. If after 6 weeks no one has mentioned the missing report, it may be something to strategically quit. If doing so goes too far out of your comfort zone, send out a password-protected report. If nobody asks for the password, draw your own conclusions.

How to Apply Strategic Quitting in Your Job

Taking yourself out of the equation is the ultimate form of strategic quitting. It means that you work hard to make yourself redundant. If you make yourself redundant and reduce the effort required by your current job, you can spend more time working on your job. This action will massively boost your ability to achieve big growth goals and accelerate your career. To make matters simple, there are only three ways to apply strategic quitting as individual leaders.

The first is to *delegate*. In the classic sense, delegation means handing down work to your employees, freeing up your time to focus on more important things. This is actually a good definition of management and, though valuable, is only one part of the story. An even better approach is to give something that is work to you to someone else who considers it play. The idea is that we are all wired differently. For example, each year thousands of people sign up at universities to become dentists. For many of us, being a dentist is probably not an attractive profession. Think of fast-moving, high-pitched drills, mini fountains of blood and fearful, moaning patients. Yet, this picture is very different for our aspiring dentists, who seem to love the work! When people do the work they love, they tend to be very good at it and view it as play. This is the road to high-performance teams in which each individual operates in the field of his or her strengths.

The second way to apply strategic quitting is by *elimination.* The worst use of your time isn't doing things inefficiently, but doing what shouldn't be done in the first place. In view of our discussion about goal achieving, the obvious candidates to eliminate are activities that simply don't support progress on your most important goals.

The third way is to *outsource,* which means handing down an activity to a specialized third party so you can focus your precious effort on achieving your big goals. Outsourcing can be very straightforward, but also has a subtle application for people trained as engineers. It's possible to outsource an activity to a process. If you program a recurring data analysis in a spreadsheet, suddenly this activity is outsourced to an efficient process.

Executive Question

Where can you use your engineering strengths to delegate, eliminate, and outsource to free up time for yourself and focus on marketing, innovation, and strategy?

Summary and What's Next

In order to maintain momentum and continue to execute activities to achieve your goals, you must focus on strategic quitting: Doing more is not the answer to too much to do. Instead, you must free up time, money, and energy, which can be used elsewhere. This is necessary to achieve your strategic goals, develop your organization, and accelerate your career. Reality-based thinking helps you apply the 80/20 rule to achieve the biggest impact with the least amount of effort, both for yourself and for the organization. Process design helps you apply strategic quitting proactively and systematically.

The next chapter will discuss how to overcome inaccurate thinking and provide proper judgment to keep from getting bogged down by the thinking biases that are common in leaders with engineering backgrounds.

External Perspective

Interview of Aloys Kregting, CIO, AkzoNobel

What Has Been the Most Fascinating Aspect of Business Leadership for You?

How can you initiate collective change with a big group of people? Often the technological changes are swift, yet a group of people will generally change slowly. To deal with this, you need to appeal to the two parts of the human brain. First of all, the story must be rationally sound. Second, it must be emotionally engaging. Generally speaking, leaders with an engineering background can successfully deal with change by using two strengths. They like procedures, which makes things logically sound and they like to play in a team, which facilitates emotional engagement.

What Are Some of the Most Important Behaviors for Business Leaders with an Engineering Background to Improve their Effectiveness?

As a CIO, I once received one of the biggest compliments from a CEO: He told me that I had the ability to demystify IT. What he appreciated was my ability to use language and terminology, which aligned with where the company was heading. A message contains both content and packaging. Successful business leaders with an engineering background are not only able to focus on how their efforts will help the explicit and implicit goals of the company, but are also able to frame this in the language of their peers and bosses.

What Are Some of the Most Important Behaviors that Leaders with an Engineering Background need to Unlearn to Improve their Effectiveness?

Don't focus on perfection. Often 80 percent is good enough. For example, will a further improvement in a customer satisfaction system really help the organization further, or is it better to spend time and energy somewhere else? This requires opening your eyes to other functions in the organization and the willingness to step out of your own silo.

Which Trends Do You See that May Be Relevant for Leaders with an Engineering Background to have a Bigger Impact in the Future?

I believe that the application of robotics and artificial intelligence will have a huge impact on business processes. For example, in the United Kingdom, computer algorithms have a better track record of predicting the outcome of legal cases, than expert opinions. This means that explicit knowledge is becoming less important in the future. Business leaders with an engineering background will have an advantage, because they drive and understand technology. However, engineers who want to grow as a business leader will need to make the shift from specialist—knowing a lot of a few things, to generalist—knowing little about many things. Once they make this shift, they become a very valuable connector.

What Is Your Approach to Learning and Improving as a Business Leader Yourself?

I was working for a CEO and he told me once that we must assume there is more intelligence and knowledge outside our company than inside our company. To me, learning means a constant focus on the external world. For example, I'm a member of the Research Board: a network group consisting of senior-level CIOs. In this way, I'm actively expanding my horizon together with my peers. I do the same with vendors and customers.

CHAPTER 7

Improving Executive Judgment

How can leaders with an engineering background apply proper executive judgment to avoid making predictable mistakes on their way to achieving their goals?

Why Improving Executive Judgment Matters

The South Sea British stock company, founded in 1711, was granted a monopoly to trade with South America. As a result, it became massively popular with investors, leading to what historians now call the South Sea bubble. Blinded by greed, investors were willing to throw more and more money to obtain the coveted shares. When the bubble eventually burst, it left many investors with an empty wallet and a broken dream. Bubbles happen all the time, yet it was remarkable that even smart people who should have known better were sucked in. One victim was no less than Sir Isaac Newton.

The pattern of smart people making stupid decisions is a consistent theme in history. Most recent examples are Enron, WorldCom, and the Bernie Madoff scam, where the list of investors who got duped is long and full of famous smart people. Clearly, smart and intelligent is not the default position of your brain; it needs to be switched on. Once you understand how to control this switch, you'll be able to embrace a smarter self to better understand reality, improve judgment, and achieve big goals.

How to Engage Your Executive Thinking Faculty

My favorite cartoon television series of all times revolved around two mice. One was called Pinky: fast, intuitive, and not always bright. The other one was called the Brain, the smart one. The objective of both mice was to conquer the world. In each episode, the plot revolved around the crazy, outlandish, but brilliant schemes that were concocted by the megalomaniacal Brain. His plans were invariably ruined by Pinky's clumsy execution. The main characters in this reoccurring drama represent a mirror to our own brains. To understand why smart people sometimes make stupid decisions, it's helpful to consider two different actors occupying our brain. One actor is called *System One*. It's intuitive and fast, and jumps to conclusions. The other is *System Two*. It's lazy and deliberate, and able to systematically and logically analyze ideas. System One is active over 95 percent of the time. For example, it helps decide in a split second whether to cross the street. System One is the intuitive operator. System Two steps in when things become more complicated, like when you need to calculate 256 × 341 in your head. System Two is the lazy executive.

In order to make decisions, System One makes use of heuristics, mental rules of thumb that are adequate most of the time. For example, the speed of an approaching car can be estimated by the sound of the engine, comparison between other moving objects in the vicinity, and general speed limit. In a split second, these data points lead to a decision to cross the street or not. Yet, sometimes the rules of thumb look good, but, upon closer examination, are simply inadequate to correctly interpret the data and make a proper judgment. These are called *biases* and are the source of many mistakes in business and in life.

For example, let's again take a look at the world of investing. The trick to successful investing is to not make mistakes. In other words, don't lose money. You make mistakes by chasing hot stocks, trying to time the market or thinking that the window of opportunity for buying a new stock is closing rapidly. Especially in a falling market, the investor who refuses to make mistakes will come out on top.

The same is true for goal achieving. When things work out well and you're smoothly sailing through the Valley of Death, you don't worry about the quality of decision making. System One, the intuitive operator, is on autopilot. However, as soon as you're about to hit a wall and System Two, the lazy executive, is actually called for, you need to increase your awareness and advance your thinking. System One on autopilot is the oil in the gearbox of execution power. However, at times System One will unconsciously start to mix the oil with sand, bringing your gearbox to a grinding halt. Effortless goal achievement, therefore, is about letting System One, your intuitive operator, run its course most of the time and quickly let System Two, the lazy executive, step in when needed.

How can you strike a balance between the two systems and use the engineering strengths of reality-based thinking, process design, and accelerated learning to engage System Two in critical moments when a higher level of executive thinking is called for?

How Reality-Based Thinking Overcomes the Fallacy of Coherent Stories

Earlier you saw the cargo cult thinking fallacy: Primitive people on remote islands replicated airfields used in World War II—for example with bamboo watchtowers and coconut helmets—in the hope that the planes would return again. By mimicking the visual clues of success, the idea is that you're able to copy the source of success. Let's extend this metaphor even further. Before they started to build their own version of an airfield, imagine that your primitive cargo cult brethren are not only monitoring the activity of the planes, but are fully aware of the scientific rules of statistical data as well. They start to observe that longer runways invite bigger planes. They also notice that sunny weather increases the chance of a plane landing. More and more data paints a more and more compelling picture of how the world works. At a certain point, the scientific evidence and correlation between actions and results become overwhelming. All data fits the story. Yet, all of a sudden, the planes stop coming. Little do the primitive people know that the peace treaty between the United States and Japan has made strategic use of remote airfield activities obsolete. Thus, the planes simply stop coming even on sunny days. Our primitive brethren embraced a proper, even scientific story. Yet, they completely missed the bigger picture. This fallacy is called *scientism*: With all data available, you build a coherent story that is neat, plausible, and spectacularly wrong.

Often examples of scientism and the lure of coherent stories are found in corporate strategies. A powerful case is presented based on a tight story with ample data, which of course ends with big business success, usually represented by some form of hockey stick on a colorful diagram. To make proper judgment around strategy plans and corporate goals, you therefore need to apply reality-based thinking and look for what's missing instead.

Executive Questions

To avoid being blinded by coherent stories, improve executive judgment, and find missing parts of a corporate strategy, you need to ask:

- What else can explain these data points? This question uncovers lack of alternative explanations for stated facts.
- What needs to happen to ruin this strategy? This information points to vague or missing assumptions.
- Who has tried before and has failed? This knowledge will prevent you from ignoring historic trends and developments.
- Why are you using impossibly accurate numbers (like market share will grow to 24.89 percent in 5 years, really?). This question challenges mindless extrapolation of uncertain data.

How Reality-Based Thinking Overcomes Cognitive Dissonance

An interesting feature of System One is that it's perfectly able to stubbornly hold on to preexisting beliefs, even in the face of massive contrary evidence.

On December 21, 1954, dozens of individuals, headed by Dorothy Martin, sat in a room in Chicago, awaiting the apocalypse promised by the Clarion alien civilization. They were members of a doomsday cult, which predicted the end of the world at midnight that day. Hours after midnight nothing catastrophic had happened. Strangely enough, after the prophesy failed to materialize, the cult members became even more convinced of the cult's assumption. The psychologists labeled this irrational belief *cognitive dissonance.*

Cognitive dissonance is a widespread phenomenon, where decision makers and leaders cling to deeply held preexisting beliefs, such as doomsday beliefs, even in the face of massive contrary evidence. One example of a doomsday belief is the population bomb, a widely held scientific belief started in the 1960s, which predicted overpopulation would make the earth uninhabitable somewhere around the year 2000. In hindsight, this idea was neat, plausible, and spectacularly wrong. Mankind is still here, with more people than imagined, surrounded by more abundance than ever.

Doomsday thinking is not limited to the venerable halls of science. For example, in business, we have seen massive panic and frantic action about the change to a new millennium (Y2K). On January 1, 2000, the calendar change would lead to software disasters and bring many vital systems in the world to its knees. This fear was a dud as well. Apart from massive celebrations, nothing big happened that night. It was highly lucrative for the IT industry though, as there is always a group that benefits from excessive fear-mongering to make profits of doom.

You can look back and laugh at the silliness of the past, but doomsday thinking may play a prominent role in your business as well. If you honestly want to know whether you're guilty of doomsday thinking as a guiding business principle, ask yourself what disaster stories you tell your clients or employees to move them to take action. Then stop this destructive habit and focus on having an honest conversation about risks and rewards instead. Doomsday language undermines your credibility as a leader and, if used as a basis for doing business, erodes trust, and will set you up for failure in the long run.

Often, doomsday thinking, or its opposite counterpart *baseless exuberance*, is driven by our inability to:

- Understand small or big chances. This inability is why a statement like, "the survival rate of cancer is 97 percent," often feels very different from a similar statement that says that the mortality rate of cancer is 3 percent. However, both statements signal the same piece of data,.
- Have a good feel of small or big numbers. For example, what does the total government debt of $20 trillion actually mean? A neat trick to understand numbers is to interpret numbers in a timeline. To understand how much a trillion actually is, imagine the following.

If 1 equals 1 second, then:
- 1 million equals approximately 12 days.
- 1 billion equals approximately 32 years.
- 1 trillion equals more than 31,000 years.

Doomsday beliefs—especially the ones using the fig leaf of scientific truth—have, historically speaking, been consistently wrong and therefore need to be viewed with the greatest level of skepticism. It's best to adhere to the first rule of thoughtful leadership: When prophets of doom predict the end of the world, they probably want to sell you something.

How Reality-Based Thinking Overcomes the Semmelweis Reflex

Another System One thinking bias that sometimes interferes with the reality principle and clouds your thinking is the *Semmelweis reflex*. As a young doctor in Vienna, Ignaz Semmelweis observed that the habit of washing hands by the medical staff significantly decreased the mortality rate of women giving birth in the Vienna hospital. Since bacteria would be discovered by Louis Pasteur only decades later, he was unable to scientifically explain his findings and as a result was scorned by the established medical community. Instead of eternal fame, his standing amongst his peers literally washed away. He spent the last weeks of his tragic life in a mental hospital, driven mad by his inability to instill simple medical habits to save many lives. Instead of being a towering giant of human ingenuity and advancement, he became an ignominious footnote in the history books.

The Semmelweis reflex is a metaphor for the rejection of new knowledge because it contradicts existing norms, beliefs, or paradigms. It's a form of mental myopia that can spell doom, even for the most successful organizations. Take, for instance, a paradigm of the financial industry. The dominant idea for success in the stock market has always been the ability to pick the right stocks and time the market. This ability explains the popularity of hedge funds, CNBC, and celebrity mutual fund managers. What if picking the right stocks and timing the market are governed much more by luck than skill? It would mean that investing success is driven by simply buying and holding a diversified indexed stock portfolio for a long time. Case in point: Recent research on stock investment success says that stock management is the biggest cause of stock investing underperformance. They actually found that people who had forgotten they had opened a stock investment account in the past performed only second best. Those who had opened an investment account and didn't touch it because they had died did the best . . . .

For leaders with engineering backgrounds, the best way to combat mental myopia is to be aware of your own biases regarding coherent stories and the Semmelweis reflex. Then, filter plans and predictions through the lens of reality-based thinking. If past predictions didn't match past reality, then it's most likely that future predictions in this area are simply wrong as well.

How Process Design Overcomes Mental Substitution

A few years ago, I was in charge of recommending the location of a large production facility to a CEO. The investments were significant. The company already owned a smaller production facility. While reviewing the different alternatives, something interesting happened. When I asked several stakeholders the question, "Which location would be best for the business?," many argued vehemently for the existing location. When I asked why, it became clear they were convinced that expanding the existing facility would result in the least amount of hassle. They didn't answer the original question, "Which location would be best for the business?," but instead answered a different, easier question, "Which location decision would be easiest to execute?"

Replacing a difficult question with an easier one is called *mental substitution*, which is common in business. For example, the question, "How happy are you with the performance of an individual?" is often replaced with another easier question, "How much do you like the individual?"

You can overcome the mental substitution fallacy in judgment through a systematic approach to evaluate alternatives. An excellent process to apply this approach is using a cause and effect (C and E) matrix.

Practical Application

A cause and effect (C and E) matrix is a decision-making tool to overcome mental substitution and improve executive judgment. Here's how it works:

- Frame the problem as a set of alternatives. For example, should you open a new office in the Asian, European, or US market, or simply do nothing?
- Define the decision-making criteria, such as speed, cost, investment size, market, etc.
- Weigh the importance of each decision-making criterion, with 1 being the lowest weight and 10 the highest.
- Grade alternatives to each criteria. Use the numbers 1 (low), 3 (medium), or 9 (high).
- Calculate weight × grade and then calculate the sum of all scores for each of the alternatives.
- The highest-scoring alternative is the default decision. Carefully review other reasons you shouldn't pick the default position.

You've now minimized the chance of mental substitution and are ready to make a better decision.

How Accelerated Learning Overcomes the Planning Fallacy

The *probability* of an outcome is driven by statistics: The chance of winning at roulette in a casino while only betting on black and white is less than 50 percent. The colorless number 0 tilts the bigger chance of winning toward the house. The problem arises when you confuse statistical probability of an outcome with the *plausibility* of the same outcome. For example, the chance, or probability, of winning the lottery is extremely small. To put things in perspective, statistically you're more likely to have a fatal accident on your way to buying a ticket for the lottery than of actually winning the power ball. Winning this lottery is most certainly plausible, though. After all, there have been quite some power ball winners. That's why people continue to buy lottery tickets.

The replacement of probability with plausibility is a major mistake when trying to achieve big business goals. This truth is often very apparent in project planning. Fueled by unwarranted optimism, businesses often commit to aggressive and overly optimistic timelines: a typical example of the planning fallacy. How many initiatives are delivered in time, in spec, and on budget in your organization? Sometimes, the planning fallacy is used deliberately to get, for example, funding for a mediocre project approved. If the project proposal would have contained more realistic numbers, it would never have passed the approval hurdle.

Knowing this fallacy, what can you do to improve decision making and accelerate learning to make more accurate judgments about future achievements? The answer is *baseline thinking,* introduced in Chapter 4: always start your endeavor with an objective baseline to estimate the chance of success and then honestly assess your own skill level to judge your actual chance accordingly. For example, the majority of all mergers and acquisitions don't achieve their intended goals. If your company has caught a serious case of acquisition fever, start with a failure base rate, for example, 70 percent. Then ask if your skills and track record warrant moving up or down the failure rate scale. Naturally this exercise will be refreshing, enlightening, and sobering. You're probably not as skilled and accomplished as you may have thought initially: In many cases this understanding will save the company a lot of money.

Knowing when to engage System Two and apply baseline thinking is hard. Many business leaders are in love with doing mergers and acquisitions. Even if they know the statistics, they still somehow believe the outcomes will not apply to them. It requires a curious mindset, scan the outside world for information, and use the information to accelerate your understanding of the issue.

How Accelerated Learning Overcomes Myopic Thinking

Do you want to increase the bottom line of your business? If so, how can you sell more to existing and new customers? You can also frame this differently: how can you create more value for existing and new customers? In both cases, the outcome may be the same, yet the perspective is different. Changing perspective by asking different questions is called framing and, in this case, it helps to look at different solutions to increase your bottom line.

Framing is especially useful when looking for ways to accelerate innovation. Every business or profession has industry or professional standards also known as *norms*. Examples of these norms are:

- Cardboard, paper, or plastic is virtually always used to protect packages sent by mail.
- The proper sequence in a restaurant is to enter, eat, and pay.
- Plumbers get paid when they need to fix the drain of your house. They are not paid at times when the plumbing works perfectly.

Norm is an abbreviation for *normal*. If you do what is normal in your industry or profession, you do what everybody is doing. You will also get the outcomes everybody is getting. These outcomes are generally boring and predictable System One results. Instead, you want extraordinary results by engaging System Two, your lazy executive brain.

One way to rapidly innovate therefore starts with framing the right question focused on breaking standards in your industry. For instance, if you are in the computer business, a question could be, "What if I could no longer sell computers at physical stores?" If you think long and hard, you would probably come up with an innovative business approach as pioneered by Dell.

It's interesting that selling things without a physical store has been applied in other industries than the computer industry. Take for example selling gadgets through TV shopping channels, which typically run in the middle of the night. In other words, the fastest way to innovate is to simply look for and apply different standards from other industries or professions.

A second way to use framing to innovate is to look for what is actually missing. During World War II, a group of statisticians was asked to find ways to reduce the number of American airplanes that didn't return from missions. After studying bullet-hole patterns in aircrafts that returned from missions, the idea was to add more armor to the areas of the planes where they had been hit the most—wings, fuel system, and fuselage—but, oddly enough, not on the engines, which had the smallest number of bullet holes per square meter. Then, one statistician asked an interesting question: Where were the missing bullet holes—the ones that would be all over the engine if bullets were equally distributed? The answer was obvious: The missing bullet holes were on the planes that had been shot down and hadn't returned. The critical part of a plane was not where most of the bullet holes were on the returning planes. It was where the bullet holes were on the planes that were shot down. For a business leader, an interesting question is therefore: "Where are the missing bullet holes in my company?" Or, applied to customers, "What is the biggest irritation of a typical customer in our business, and how can we innovate to take this annoyance away?" This analysis has led to interesting concepts like that of the now defunct carmaker Saturn—a car that could be bought only for a fixed price, with no price negotiation necessary or even allowed.

Framing is an effective way for leaders with an engineering background to overcome myopic thinking and drive innovation in their companies and achieve big goals. By applying accelerated learning and actively broadening their skills and experience, they are also exposed to different standards and thinking frames. Applying these standards in their own environments enhances their abilities to innovate as leaders. When Henry Ford developed the assembly line, little did he know that 100 years later this idea would be applied to fast-food chains all over the world.

How to Implement a Process to Avoid Mistakes

The biases covered in this chapter can wreak havoc while you move toward your goals. Once you become aware of the typical signs of System One biases, it will be much easier to deliberately activate System Two and engage in executive thinking. An even better way to get rid of roadblocks from thinking biases is to prevent them from occurring in the first place.

A powerful tool for a leader to improve executive judgment is the *pre-mortem exercise*. A pre-mortem is the reversal of a project post mortem, which identifies mistakes after a project has failed. In a pre-mortem, however, you identify the major causes of project failure in a creative way before the start of a project by imagining the project has already failed. This exercise enables you to eliminate roadblocks and ensure a smooth execution.

Practical Application

This is how to execute a pre-mortem exercise to avoid critical mistakes and ensure smooth project execution:

- Imagine 5 to 10 years in the future. Your project has failed so miserably that you've been asked for an interview by the *Wall Street Journal* to provide an in-depth analysis of why the initiative failed.
- Divide the project team into small subgroups to discuss what should be said in the interview.
- All subgroups report on what they discussed. The feedback should give a clear picture of the main obstacles. Steps to eliminate these obstacles can then be incorporated into the project design from the start.
- Conduct a pre-mortem with a group of external subject experts, which will not only provide fresh insights regarding risks, but also help you quickly identify hidden opportunities. This knowledge will be a great eye-opener and help develop alternatives for achieving your major goals.

Summary and What's Next

As a business leader, while executing the activities to achieve your goal, it's essential to apply proper judgment and avoid preventable mistakes. Most of the time, it's sufficient to rely on System One, the intuitive operator, to make thousands of tiny daily decisions. However, there will be critical moments when executive thinking by System Two, the lazy executive, is required. Your strengths—reality-based thinking, process design, and accelerated learning—provide a framework to not only notice these critical moments, but improve your judgment as well. Conducting a pre-mortem before committing to a big goal is an effective way to actively use your executive thinking power to prevent many avoidable mistakes.

Now that you understand the role of executive thinking to improve judgment while executing your goals, in the next chapter, you will get a chance to take a closer look at adverse habits that mask your unique strengths and slow down execution.

External Perspective

Stépan Breedveld, Senior Partner and Managing Director at The Boston Consulting Group (BCG)

Which Trends Do You See that May Be Relevant for Leaders with an Engineering Background to Have a Bigger Impact in the Future?

I have noticed there are many CEOs with a technical and/or analytical background. This doesn't surprise me, since technological developments, such as digitalization, are only accelerating. Furthermore, the time horizon of a business leader is getting shorter as well. A long-term time frame used to be 10 years; now it's 3 years or even less. Decision making is therefore becoming more complex and at the same time requires more speed. Thus, in the future, the effectiveness of business leaders will increasingly be determined both by leadership and by content knowledge.

What Are Some of the Most Important Behaviors for Business Leaders with an Engineering Background to Improve their Effectiveness?

A core activity of a leader is the ability to move an entire organization. This skill requires two things. First, a leader must be able to clarify the direction of an organization. Second, a leader must be able to inspire the entire organization to move faster. To facilitate this process, you therefore need to have a conversation, which starts with understanding the purpose of an organization. This insight is especially important in difficult times. People can handle many setbacks, as long as the purpose of their work is clear. Understanding the purpose is not only true for an organization, but applies on a deep personal level for any leader. When I was CEO of Ordina, one of the most interesting questions I was once asked was: "Why are your working here?"

(continued)

Second, I think leaders should focus on their strengths and be aware of their weaknesses. This is how they can build a good team: Different people with different strengths, covering each other's weaknesses. Unfortunately, this diversity doesn't always happen. Sometimes, leaders with engineering backgrounds surround themselves with team members who have the same profile, which tends to limit conversations to content only.

Finally, business leaders need to be selective with receiving feedback. As a CEO, you are often in the spotlight and will receive input from many people. You have to carefully choose which feedback is important and which feedback should be ignored.

What Are Some of the Most Important Behaviors that Leaders with Engineering Backgrounds Need to Unlearn to Improve their Effectiveness?

One thing I learned as a leader was to find a balance between content and connection. Engineers tend to love content. Yet, being an effective leader is more than that. The future competitive advantage of a company is much more than having a superior strategy. After all, we can buy a strategy in the marketplace. What will become more important is the vision, mission, and execution power of the strategy, which is driven by all things human: culture, relationship, etc. This understanding is what separates the successful from the less successful companies.

What Is Your Approach to Learning and Improving as a Business Leader Yourself?

My objective is not to strive for perfection in all dimensions, but to focus on what I'm good at. I can easily distinguish the important and the not so important. I keep calm, even if things become chaotic. I am easily bored and always curious, which helps me to grow as a leader. Finally, one of the key things is to take care of your health. Leadership at the highest level requires an enormous amount of energy. You will burn out quickly if you don't manage this consciously.

CHAPTER 8

Eliminating Adverse Habits

How can leaders with an engineering background become aware and get rid of adverse habits that mask unique strengths and impair the execution of actions toward their goals?

Why Eliminating Adverse Habits Matters

The Roman comic dramatist Terence once said it's important to have moderation in all things. We know that water is important for our body, but drinking more than 6 L within an hour will kill you. It's possible to have too much of a good thing (chocolate may be the exception though). If leaders with engineering backgrounds aren't careful, they run the risk of applying their strengths to the extreme limit under the wrong circumstances. As a result, their strengths may actually be masked and eliminated, which may have a detrimental effect on achieving big goals. I call these unhelpful applications of strengths *Kryptonite habits*, after the famous fictional substance Kryptonite, which was able to completely nullify Superman's superpowers.

A characteristic of Kryptonite habits is that their application is unconscious, a System One activity. Their effects are contextual and typically mask your strengths as a business leader. For example, the reality principle will work magic when it comes to making proper business decisions. It can be annoying and counterproductive when it interferes with a gripping tale of an imaginative movie: You know that laser cannons don't make sound in space, yet you must suspend your disbelief to still enjoy the thunderous sound effects of a *Star Wars* space battle. Therefore, it's important to use your strengths as a focused rapier, not as a crude bludgeon.

Your focus on getting rid of Kryptonite habits differs from focusing on improving weaknesses. Kryptonite habits mask strengths. Therefore, the difference is that getting rid of Kryptonite habits will actually increase your strengths, while a focus on improving weaknesses tries to build new strengths on barren ground. A race car will go faster with better tires. Inferior tires will mask the car's performance. A race car is not a family hauler though, so even if you would equip it with a tow bar to compensate its weaknesses, it will still be a lousy vehicle for family trips.

Thus, it's important to become aware and get rid of several notorious Kryptonite habits, which typically plague even the most successful leaders with engineering background. All of these habits are based on pushing your strengths of reality-based thinking, process design, and accelerated learning too far, or applying these strengths under the wrong circumstances.

In this chapter, I have compiled a list of 10 typical unhelpful behaviors of leaders with engineering background, which may mask strengths. All these behaviors are framed with metaphors, because this approach makes your own awareness of the typical moments when you show these behaviors much easier. Furthermore, it provides a powerful framework to address these behaviors in others.

How to Avoid Butterflies in the Wrong Stomach

A big mistake is to fall in love with your processes or product, instead of falling in love with the best results for your customers. Although you may have invested time and money in a particular process, in the end it's only the results that count. If a process doesn't work, stop tinkering, apply strategic quitting, and pull the plug. Letting go to achieve better results is hard. It's also necessary. Often letting go of a big initiative feels like losing, especially when you've invested time and energy in getting people enthusiastic about the results.

A prominent example of falling in love with processes instead of results is the drive to outsource IT and finance to cheaper places in the world. Though the business case is often attractive, even a no-brainer, many companies have found that the benefits are much more limited and the added headaches are exponentially worse than initially anticipated. It's therefore no surprise that General Motors made waves when it recently announced it would insource a majority of its IT operations to delivery centers in the United States.

The best remedy to counter the *having butterflies in the wrong stomach effect* is to define go/no go criteria before proceeding to a next milestone or course of action. For example, in project management, it is a best practice to use predetermined criteria in order to pass to the next project stage. This habit forces you to think of important criteria to abandon a project before you commit too many resources.

Executive Question

What needs to happen to abandon your most important initiative? How do you check this progress on a regular basis?

How to Avoid Foie Gras Persuasion

Foie gras is a French delicacy made by force-feeding geese to exponentially grow their livers. Though foie gras tastes excellent, it makes the geese deeply unhappy. Have you ever been guilty of force-feeding your ideas to others? Your ideas and insights may be logical and reality-based yet remain unconvincing. The reason is that perception is reality, and perception is driven by filters that determine how you see the world. If you want to bring others to your point of view, stop lecturing and start asking questions.

To avoid falling into the foie gras persuasion trap, insist on discussing two questions when persuading others to help you achieve your goal:

- Under what circumstances would this goal be important to you as well?
- What else would suddenly be possible if you would succeed with this goal?

Once, I proposed a significant, unplanned investment to reduce a huge business risk in our manufacturing operation. This was of course difficult. Then I asked these two question and the CEO realized that the investment would make him sleep much better at night. All of a sudden, the *What's-in-it-for-me* (Wiifm) became obvious for him. We didn't need more logical arguments, and the project was quickly approved.

How to Avoid Being Lost in Logic

Logic makes people think, while emotion makes them act. Often more reality-based logic is not the answer to persuade others. Instead, different ingredients, such as appealing to emotions, are necessary. If three good arguments won't do, 10 additional mediocre arguments won't help either. We can take a page from the playbook of lawyers. Court scenes on television are typically dramatized, but often contain a grain of truth. We never see a case led by insurmountable logic. We always see the logical arguments used to support the main emotional arguments.

Therefore, adopt the habit of never giving more than three logical arguments, which should be your best. Any added weaker arguments would be the focus of rebuttal and would seriously weaken your case.

How to Avoid Perfection before Production

A main reason people procrastinate to make a decision and bring an imperfect result to the world is the fear of missing out on something important. In other words, they believe that spending a little more energy, thought, or effort might massively increase their chances of success. I was brought in by a company with a horrible safety record. My assignment was to improve its performance. A short audit revealed significant deviations in core safety processes throughout the entire organization. When I argued that we should focus on this quickly, the initial reaction was pushback. To make changes in a sustainable way, shouldn't we look at a new organizational model first? I realized that this company had a culture where looking for perfection was actually an excuse to do nothing and preserve the status quo. When a patient is in critical condition and brought into the emergency room, the first objective of a doctor is to stabilize the patient. Only then can a more rigorous approach help improve the patient's condition.

Typical signs that an organization uses the excuse of perfection to avoid doing actual work and expose itself to risk of failure are:

- Frequent meetings without action lists and lack of accountability for taking actions.
- The language of the procrastinator:
  - Let's review additional alternatives.
  - Let's decide not to decide.
  - We need more information.
  - Let's organize a meeting to review where we are.
  - Shouldn't we focus on something else as well?
  - Let's conduct a benchmark.
- An obsession with asking why. The idea is that organizations with powerful why's are able to execute big goals more smoothly. However, the quest for why can often paralyze an organization. When in front of an incoming train, asking why is the wrong course of action. As a leader, it's important to find a balance between asking why and moving into action mode, the how and the what.

For engineers, nothing is more beautiful than designing a smooth, harmonious, and almost magical process before bringing it to the real world. Leave that quest to your hobbies. In the business world, your focus on speed and functionality trumps beauty every time.

How to Avoid Gilding the Lily

Many die with their music still inside. Thus, creative expression is often done in isolation. You wait till you're sure your efforts rise immediately to the top of the food chain. However, realize that actual improvement is based on feedback from the outside world. You cannot learn and look good at the same time. If you take driving lessons, it is unrealistic to morph into an outstanding driver the very moment you sit behind the wheel for the first time. For engineers, solving problems by 80 percent is often good enough for a business to move ahead and thrive. When I was a young process engineer, I was tasked to build a spreadsheet to help optimize a chemical plant. The spreadsheet was done quickly, but I was so enthusiastic that I decided to extend my work and build a state-of-the-art user interface. After weeks of work, my interface was launched. Yet, it soon became clear that it was irrelevant for the operators. What mattered was the data. The operators built their own shortcut to reach the data, while ignoring the interface I had created.

Executive Question

Where do you gild the lily and allow your organization to continue tinkering with what actually works well?

The final few benefits are always irrelevant to others. If something is good enough, simply move on.

How to Avoid Landing without Skill

Edward Howard Armstrong was a brilliant engineer who single handedly invented FM radio technology. To most of us, however, his massive contribution to science and engineering is unknown. He combined absolute brilliance with a rough and difficult personality, which made him simply unable to win powerful people over to help him to implement his ideas. Though his inventions continue to live on, the name Edward Howard Armstrong remains a small footnote in the history books of science.

Comparing his life with people like Henry Ford, Nicola Tesla, and Thomas Edison, it is clear that, while having a similar scientific brilliance, all of these great men had the ability to persuade powerful people to support their causes.

Brilliance thrives in a nurturing environment, which, however, is not always obvious. Think of the last time you triumphantly made a devastating and uncomfortable yet excellent point in your staff meeting and to your dismay, people became upset, cranky, and unresponsive. Often, this result is not because your point is wrong, but the way you addressed the issue was blunt and unhelpful. Landing a plane in one piece is good. Avoiding a cabin full of frightened passengers suffering from nausea is better.

I was hired by a CEO to help one of his direct reports who made the numbers but somehow was not liked by his peers. While observing his behavior, it became apparent he possessed a keen talent to quickly understand an issue. Yet, addressing the issue in a subtle way was much more difficult for him. His style was confrontational, hammering on clarity, and backing others in a corner. This habit made him completely ineffective as a persuader.

People don't like to lose face. Therefore, it's important to always provide a gracious way out. His focus on boxing people in made him unpopular.

As a business leader, it's helpful to understand military strategy. Sun Tzu, the famous Chinese general, already understood that an army with no means of escape will fight to the death. In the end, it's about proper judgment. How can you apply massive pressure to get things done and at the same time provide a tactical way out to help your employees save face? Your skill at accelerated learning may help you to be ahead of the issues. Yet, this requires a thoughtful approach to get others on board as well.

I was able to help the executive by focusing on these questions:

- Which goal do you ultimately want to achieve?
- Was your behavior effective in moving toward that goal?
- What would you do differently next time?

Executive Question

In your next interaction, when should you skip the sledge hammer and apply tact and empathy to bring your message across?

How to Avoid Excessive Ahabism

The downfall of Captain Ahab, the protagonist of Moby Dick, became his obsession with catching the white whale. There is a fine line between admirable persistence and block-headed tenacity. If you're the only one left on the barricades, it's time to leave and focus your energy on something else.

We all recognize moments when we were so obsessed with achieving a goal, that somehow along the way we forgot the reason why. This is the definition of a fanatic. Leaders sometimes fall into the excessive Ahabism trap. Because the goal is based on reality and they have neat process in place to achieve the goal, they may miss signals that conditions have changed. These are typical signs that you may be chasing a white whale:

- The company is so focused on market share that margins rapidly erode and financial results deteriorate. The old joke is that a

company may have negative margins, but they make it up with additional volume.
- Assumptions for key strategic projects are no longer reviewed on a regular basis. Even new people are quickly drawn into action and are no longer curious as to why certain things are done.
- The organization becomes blind to alternatives. More resources are poured into failing projects, while these resources may have been better used elsewhere. This is called the *sunk cost* fallacy and is one of the main reasons it's so difficult to abandon failing projects.

Executive Question

How do you know you have crossed the line between admirable persistence and block-headed tenacity?

How to Avoid Winners Addiction

When you're a debating champion, you run the risk of seeing every human interaction as a debate. If you do, you will become lonely very quickly. The same is true for engineers. If you wield the scepter of logic anywhere, anytime, anyplace to batter your coworkers into submission, you may be right, but won't be successful. Pick your battles carefully and play along with the rest. It's more important to be effective than to be right.

The battles that matter most help you and the organization move toward the most important goals. You may not know everything, but if you can honestly admit you're sometimes wrong, you will become a stronger leader. This is often difficult for leaders trained as engineers. After all, you're educated to believe there is often only one way to solve a scientific problem: The complex calculation governing the trajectory of a space rocket is either right or wrong. There is no in between. This type of science is digital—either 1 or 0.

The problem arises when we confuse business judgment with hard, digital science. Judgment involves where to invest, who to hire, which products to develop, etcetera. In this case, there are multiple ways to achieve the desired results. When studying science as an engineer, you had to prove you knew the right answer in order to succeed. Proving is no longer necessary when you move to business leadership. The rules have changed. Now you need to develop and choose between a plethora of good decisions.

I once worked closely with a brilliant scientist to develop a mathematical model of a complex chemical reactor. He was a nice guy, whose main satisfaction was to be right in the modeling field. That was a good thing. However, he extended this behavior—the insistence to be right all the time—to matters of strategy, project execution, and people judgment. He became opinionated, argumentative, and estranged from the team. This lone wolf behavior resulted in the decision to cut him loose from the project.

Executive Question

Where are you trying to win, when this area is actually irrelevant for your success as a business leader?

How to Avoid Becoming a Solution Monopolist

There are many alternatives to achieve a goal. Instead of dismissing options from others, sometimes it's better to focus on how to make the alternatives from others work better. It's better to be known as a highway builder than a toll road monopolist.

This important reason is why diverse teams tend to get better results than nondiverse teams. Keep in mind that diversity in this case means having different perspectives. For example, one of the least diverse teams can be found in niche studies in academia. Think of exobiology faculties, which attract those who share an essential similar perspective: They believe in life outside our planet, and different opinions in this area are frowned upon.

Diversity in itself, however, isn't enough. There must be a common, inclusive ground of core values for all team members to adhere to. You may be unique because you consider respectful communication a luxury. This doesn't make you a diverse team player. It makes you a destructive influence.

How to Avoid Mensa Madness

Membership in the Mensa organization is based on meeting a certain intelligence standard. Mensa members therefore believe they are smart people. Like Mensa members, business leaders with an engineering background generally believe they are smart people too. However, sometimes they exhibit an uncontrollable urge to proudly let the world know they are smart, right, and know much more than you. This attitude often shifts the interaction with colleagues and clients from how much they can help to how much they know, which is what I call *Mensa madness*.

Recently, I decided to buy a new TV. I knew exactly what I wanted. However, the sales professional couldn't help himself, and continued to explain every single minute detail of this particular model. He was in love with his knowledge. I, on the other hand, quickly became exhausted. I politely mentioned that I would think about it, walked out of the store and bought the TV online. If you recognize the destructive habit of Mensa madness in yourself, simply stop it. A powerful lesson of high performance is it's better to be effective than look smart.

Executive Question

Where do you try to look smart instead of being effective as a business leader?

Table 8.1 gives an overview of the 10 Kryptonite habits of leaders with an engineering background and how they influence organizational effectiveness.

Summary and What's Next

This chapter has shown that the ability to achieve big goals starts not only with a focus on strengths, but, at the same time, with the elimination of adverse and often unconscious habits that nullify strengths. This knowledge will help you not only get started, but keep going when things become difficult. It's much easier to recognize Kryptonite habits in others than in yourself. The Romans had a clever process to deal with the problem of Kryptonite habits. They often had huge parades to celebrate

Table 8.1 The impact of Kryptonite habits on organizational effectiveness

Kryptonite habit	Impact on organizational effectiveness
Butterflies in the wrong stomach	Misalignment on goals
Foie gras persuasion	Loss of emotional connection to goals
Lost in logic	Decrease of quality of judgment
Perfection before production	Decrease of execution power
Gilding the lily	Missed opportunities
Landing without skill	Decrease of trust
Excessive Ahabism	Misaligned resources
Winners addiction	Loss of cooperation
Solution monopolist	Loss of innovation power
Mensa madness	Loss of customer intimacy

massive victories over their enemies. The conquering general rode in a chariot. A slave stood behind him, whispering in his ear a warning: All glory is fleeting.

Now that you have seen the pitfall of using too much of your unique strengths, or using your unique strengths in the wrong environment, let's turn to the final chapter dealing with goal execution: How to build connections that will help you rapidly grow your business.

External Perspective

Interview of Erik Oostwegel, CEO and Chairman of the Management Board at Royal HaskoningDHV

What Has Been the Most Fascinating Aspect of Business Leadership for You?

I'm leading an organization with employees who are smart and highly educated. The most fascinating part of leadership is to persuade them on the basis of good arguments. Whenever possible, big decisions are based on an interactive discussion in our company. For me, this requires carefully thinking through a position and the willingness to be challenged as a leader.

(continued)

Sometimes, quick decisions are necessary. You won't have the time to carefully consult all relevant people in the organization. This reality is a difficult part of leadership, because it may lead to suboptimal decisions.

What Are Some of the Most Important Skills and Behaviors for Business Leaders with Engineering Backgrounds to Improve their Effectiveness?

As engineers, we are used to having a good grasp of the subject matter we are dealing with. Yet, because of the extensive scope of our business, we may not know all the content details anymore. In spite of this, as a leader, you still need to feel comfortable to have a content discussion. One approach is to shift this type of conversation from content to process, for instance by focusing on the project management part of the discussion.

An essential skill for leaders is to make their people comfortable. This requires three things. First, it's important to respect the expertise and talents of people. Second, the ability to absorb information quickly is critical for a leader. Finally, you need to be humble and vulnerable and admit when you know very little and trust the expertise of the other person.

What Is Your Approach to Learning and Improving as a Business Leader Yourself?

As a leader, it's very important to have *Funktionslust*: the pleasure in doing what you do best. In our business, enjoying what you do requires curiosity and an entrepreneurial spirit. It's always a pleasure to discover new things and be open to new ideas. I think that curiosity is part of the character of a good leader. I sometimes become more deeply involved in the content of projects simply because I'm curious to know things.

A disturbing trend I notice with some leaders is that they believe in the infallibility of their own judgment. As a result, they lose the courage to admit they are wrong. They are convinced they have nothing more to learn, dismiss opposing arguments, and are no longer curious to hear different perspectives. This mindset leads to hardening of attitudes and unnecessary conflicts.

CHAPTER 9

Building Client Connections

How can you build connections to increase your customer base and achieve your growth goals in the easiest way possible?

Why Client Connections Matter

No single big goal has ever been achieved in isolation. Warren Buffett, the preeminent investor, has Charlie Munger as his sidekick. Albert Einstein surrounded himself with the smartest mathematicians he could find. Steve Jobs worked closely not only with Steve Wozniak, but also with the third founder of Apple, Ronald Wayne. It's apparent that achieving big goals and crossing the Valley of Death is a team effort. That's why building and maintaining relationships drives leadership success. These relationships include your business stakeholders, such as employees, vendors, and clients. We do business and work closely with people, not organizations. Since leaders with engineering backgrounds are process thinkers, why not use these strengths to design a method to actively attract the right people? These can be employees, customers, vendors, or peers.

If you don't have a process for attracting people, you will be at the mercy of other people's processes to be attracted to you. Building business relationship should not be based on chance, but should be based on careful marketing processes. Marketing includes activities that help you to attract the right people to achieve your goals.

Every organization needs to grow. If you don't grow, you will wither and fade away. This means that every single high-paid executive in your organization must bring in new business. This includes great business leaders. In previous chapters, you have seen strategies to influence and persuade others such as your employees. In this chapter, you will discover how to build external relationships that support growth goals, which involves getting and keeping customers. After all, nothing happens until a sale is made. An effective way to strengthen client connections and attract new customers is with referrals.

How Referrals Grow Business

A referral is a recommendation of your product or service, usually from an existing client to a new prospect. There are several reasons why a referral from a trusted source is the most efficient way to achieve your growth goals as a leader as quickly, dramatically, and smoothly as possible.

First, committing to something is scary. Everyone has been burned by buying something that became a source of frustration soon afterward. The overall concern is risk. In every business transaction, risk is transferred from one party to the other and you don't want to hold the risky bag. For example, if I buy apples at the grocery store, risk is transferred from the grocery store owner to me: The grocery store owner now owns risk-free money, while I have exchanged this money for apples, which may be acid, rotten, or full of worms. This concern makes referrals powerful. Shakespeare wrote that the fragrance of the rose lingers on the hand that casts it. In other words, a referral from a trusted person automatically carries trust. And trust is the best antidote for risk. The bigger the buying decision, the more the need for trust. No one has ever chosen a brain surgeon from the Yellow Pages.

Next, with trust, the price of your product or service all of a sudden becomes much less important. If you know your babysitter will do a great job caring for your children, you're much less likely to haggle over price.

Customers referred to you not only buy easier, but buy more products and services more frequently. The conversation and mindset shift from *if* I will use your product or service to *how* shall I use your product or service.

Referred customers understand the process of referrals and will therefore be much more inclined to refer you to others. How you handle your first business transaction brings the expectation that you will always do transactions that way. Therefore, take very good care of your referral sources.

How to Build Trust

It's clear that trust is the most important component for any referral strategy to be successful. Trust means the absolute conviction that you have the best interest of the other person in mind. Building trust in a referral environment is driven by six elements:

- Reciprocation
- Consistency
- Social proof
- Liking
- Authority
- Scarcity

A core activity for business leaders with an engineering background is therefore to apply their strengths—in this case process design—to design a systematic referral process that will help them get customers to achieve their most important growth goals. These six elements are the building blocks of this process.

How to Use Reciprocation

In human relationships, we tend to mentally keep score with an *emotional bank account*. Whenever we receive something, we automatically have the urge to give something back to balance the checkbook. An effective way to use reciprocation in a referral environment is therefore to give massive value first before asking for referrals. Therefore, it's important to do what you do so well, so people can't resist telling about you. If you can turn your customers into raving fans, it's easy to turn them into raving referral fans. Two strategies will put reciprocation immediately into practice.

Practical Application

- Simply refer others first. The quickest way to get something is to give it first to others. For instance, if you want your clients to send you referrals, refer your clients to others first.
- Heap praise and recognition on your clients who have referred others to you. Make a huge deal out of the first referral. This can be mundane things, like thank you notes, or more advanced strategies, such as inviting your client to codevelop your new strategy.

How to Use Consistency

Consistent behavior enforces predictability and predictability increases the feeling of control, thus building trust. There are several ways to use consistency to improve referral rates:

Practical Application

- Educate your clients by making sure to explain your referral process in detail before asking for referrals. It will make the referral process predictable.
- Education must focus on:
  - A picture of what the ideal referral client looks like.
  - A detailed description of the process of what happens when a new referral client is introduced to you. This process includes the timing and nature of the first contact, what happens when a referral turns into a business relationship, and what happens when referrals don't turn into business relationships.
- Start with the referral in mind by creating referral expectations in the mind of a prospect before accepting the prospect as a new client. Some think the client has to experience results before referring, but this is contrary to known psychology. Instead, the new client is most enthusiastic when everything is new and when the decision to choose you is still fresh in his or her mind. Therefore, use the moment of the first sale to set the expectation that you will be asking for referrals.

How to Use Social Proof

People tend to do what their peer group is doing. Once you start gaining the trust of members in a group of peers, other members will automatically trust you more as well. Bernie Madoff could continue with his Ponzi scheme for many years, because his clients acted as referral sources to their peers.

Practical Application

You can harness the power of social proof in several ways by extending your business horizon and start to do pro bono and/or community work. This strategic approach is a form of working on your business. Often you will build relations with people who can direct you to trusted peers. These peers may turn into clients.

How to Use Liking

We do business with people we like. Your clients like you, or otherwise they wouldn't do business with you. However, they often don't refer you to others simply because doing so isn't on their radar. After all, when was the last time you spontaneously referred a trusted vendor to one of your industry peers?

Practical Application

Define the top 20 percent of your trusted vendor and customer list. Then, proactively engage these trusted partners and simply ask for referrals. You will actually do them a favor by giving them the opportunity to introduce the value of your business to valued others as well.

How to Use Authority

Authority is a powerful trigger for trust. You wouldn't necessarily follow the financial investment advice of your gardener, but when your banker talks about investment opportunities, you listen up.

Practical Application

Set up buying criteria for your type of product or business to educate your marketplace. A recent dog food commercial depicts a veterinarian in a white coat explaining why a certain mixture of vitamins is essential to keeping Bailey in top condition. This dog food, of course, is the only one that contains these essential ingredients. This trust-building advertisement was designed to educate customers, boosting the dog food rapidly to the top of dog food brands. Educating the marketplace works if you are the first one to do it and you become the benchmark in the mind of potential clients. Think of how BMW has promoted the 50-50 weight distribution as an essential criterion for a vehicle to become an "ultimate driving machine." Naturally, no car maker other than BMW has mastered the fine and elusive art of the 50-50 distribution.

How to Use Scarcity

Fashionable nightclubs use a velvet rope to manage entrance, and only the chosen can come in. The more fastidious the bouncers, the longer the line of people wanting to get in. A long line of people trying to get in builds additional trust in the quality of the nightclub. This is called the wisdom of the crowd: after all, when something is popular, it must be good. Furthermore, people want what they can't get. Think of the popularity of limited editions. Nothing becomes more attractive than limited supply. The coveted Amex Black Card is an example of how this idea is done well. You can use the awesome power of the velvet rope to your advantage in your referral strategy design.

Practical Application 1

The first variation to increase referrals by building scarcity is with mutual selection. Using this approach, first make a list of criteria that potential clients have to pass in order to do business with you. Share these criteria with new potential clients and together determine if they satisfy all criteria. Accept them as new clients only if they comply. If they don't, refer them to your competitors. In this way, you let potential clients jump through hoops to become new clients. This selectivity will make you exclusive, and exclusivity creates desire. An additional benefit is that price resistance disappears. New clients are so happy they are accepted that cost is no longer an issue. The strategy to build exclusivity as part of your business is a very effective way to offer your products and services at the highest price points.

Practical Application 2

The second variation to increase referrals by building scarcity is takeaway selling. Soup Nazi was an episode of the comedy series *Seinfeld*, which showed a long line of people anxiously awaiting their turn in a line leading to a soup restaurant. Surprisingly, the store owner was unpleasant and egregiously rude, even refusing to serve one of the Seinfeld cast. Ironically, this refusal made the soup even more attractive. In other words, human nature is somewhat perverse. We want what we can't have. Here's a practical application of takeaway selling. At some point, add a step to make it more difficult for prospects to become your clients. For instance, introduce a formal application review step to determine the final go or no go. When you do so, people will become more eager to do business with you.

Summary and What's Next

To achieve big growth goals, a business leader needs to make smart choices and build a process to maximize the impact of existing relationships and thus get new clients with the least amount of effort. This mechanism is called a referral engine and its main component is trust. With a few simple yet effective activities, a great business leader can quickly build trust and attract more customers to grow their business.

If you think you're in control, you're probably not going fast enough. In Part IV of the book, you have seen that smooth execution is not about control, but about using your strengths—reality-based thinking, process design, and accelerated learning—to anticipate and quickly overcome roadblocks and react to changes. Doing so involves strategic quitting, executive judgment, overcoming kryptonite habits and finally, building new client connections using a referral process.

In Part V, the final part of this book, we will bring the three building blocks of achieving big goals—clarity, focus, execution—together, and present an actionable blueprint to get going.

External Perspective

Interview of Paresh Bhakta, COO DSM, Engineering Plastics

What Has Been the Most Fascinating Aspect of Business Leadership for You?

The most fascinating aspect of business leadership is how much less content you use for decision making. Since the speed of business is increasing, it's no longer possible to rely on my own deep content knowledge. Therefore, I make a concerted effort on building a relationship and connection with my team. Due to the speed of change today, I need to trust my people and rely on their content knowledge to get results. The ability to judge and develop talent is greater for me today than how it was 10 years ago. Though not always a favorite thing to do, the ability to change talent quicker is important for both my team and also the individual.

The biggest transformation I have had to make going from an engineer to manager is the realization that you have less control of things than you think. As an example, when I was an engineer, I could control the outcome by controlling, or just removing, the variability of the inputs. With an understanding of our physical world, this would allow me to control by output. On the other hand, as a leader, you are a lot less in control. For example, as a COO, I'm currently leading over 1,500 people. I must judge human resource (not as predictable and controlled as laws of physics) to deliver results. Therefore, with the increase in speed and technology in our world today, I have had to develop a sense for talent and how to drive them toward the vision I have.

Good engineers may not always become great business leaders. They understand content, yet they must be able to judge the skillset of their people as well. They will fail as a leader when they dive into content and forget about making strong connections with their people. Therefore, when I begin a new job, I always start with understanding my team.

Furthermore, when I'm hiring new leaders, I am looking for two things. First, do they understand the content: This is very important to build their credibility. Second, do they have the ability to get results: not by relying on their content knowledge, but by relying on their people with content knowledge. My goal is to develop a team that works for purpose and not for a paycheck.

What Are Some of the Most Important Skills and Behaviors for Business Leaders with an Engineering Background to Improve their Effectiveness?

First, you need to have high integrity. This builds trust, which is an enabler in everything we do. Next, it's important to have a transparent method to communicate. It's also important to be direct. Finally, you must be able to condense your objectives and the objectives of your people to a maximum of three. And then lower your role to a cheerleader. If they fail, I give them support. If they succeed, I'm clapping. In this way, you're able to engage with your team through the journey. This automatically leads to respect and credibility as a leader. It also allows you to have insight into the talent that is executing your vision.

What Is Your Approach to Learning and Improving as a Business Leader Yourself?

By reading about the world around my business. As a leader in chemical industry, I read, listen, study a lot about the economics of the chemical value chain and how it integrates with new customer trends. My goal is to stay current with technology developments that can have significant impact on the future of DSM. This allows me to shape and develop a roadmap for economic success for DSM in a sustainable and meaningful way.

PART V
The Unstoppable Goal Achiever

CHAPTER 10

Goal-Achieving Blueprint

How can leaders with engineering background combine the ideas around the building blocks of goal-achieving (clarity, focus, and execution) with their strengths (reality-based thinking, process design, and accelerated learning) to design actionable blueprints to achieve big goals?

Why a Goal-Achieving Blueprint Matters

"We hoped for the best, but things turned out as usual . . .," lamented the late Russian prime minister Viktor Chernomyrdin more than 20 years ago, when he observed the weak performance of the Russian economy at that time. This blunt observation applies to both politics and business. I've encountered this on numerous occasions when big strategic business plans with lofty goals ended up in small drawers, collecting dust.

Why is it that organizations often spend a lot of energy on developing a great strategy, somehow become moderately successful but in the end actually fail to achieve their biggest goals? The problem is seldom related to the quality of the strategic goals. The biggest issue I've found is the lack of leadership with respect to execution power: the ability for an organization to consistently move toward its most important goals. This move is also known as *strategy execution*. For a business leader, strategy execution and goal-achieving are therefore synonymous.

Strategy execution is driven by senior leaders, who are generally hardworking, effective, and successful people. In a business environment that is growing ever more complex, the bar is set higher every day. *The better you get, the better you better get.* The most effective way to accomplish strategic objectives is to focus on the spear tip of a few initiatives, instead of a broad wave of many initiatives. Previous chapters have shown how important concepts like strategic quitting and building a referral machine help improve execution power and crossing the Valley of Death. This chapter will focus on using the key elements of goal achieving—clarity, focus, and execution—and the key strengths of business leaders with engineering backgrounds—reality-based thinking, process design, and accelerated learning—to build a goal-achieving blueprint to get big things done.

Why Speed and Simplicity Are Important

The twin engines of strategy execution and goal-achieving are *simplicity* and *speed*. Simplicity gives a consistent direction, also known as *true north*. With simplicity, all stakeholders know where an organization is going. One reason the German grocery chain Aldi has been able to successfully keep expanding in a crowded marketplace is simplicity in stockkeeping. It doesn't believe in multiple brands offering the same product. The one product, one brand strategy acts as a spear tip that makes shopping decisions for its clients simple.

Speed provides a sense of urgency to get moving, test new approaches, and quickly pull the plug when an approach fails. Speed is the driving force for agility and is enormously valued in the marketplace. Amazon Prime is a shining example of how speed can accelerate a business and leave competition far behind. Yet, strangely enough, examples of organizations using speed to create a competitive edge are still limited. It could be that many fear that speed decreases control. However, if you think you're in control, you're probably not going fast enough. A focus on speed is therefore a huge opportunity for leaders to make their organizations stand out in the marketplace. Figure 10.1 shows the impact of speed and simplicity on strategy execution power.

If speed and simplicity are absent, you're stuck in quicksand. You don't know where to go, which really doesn't matter because you're not moving anyway. A typical example, where being stuck in quicksand is no exception, is health care in the United States. In times past, loaded with money, there was no need for health care providers to do things differently. However, in the past two decades, money has become scarce, and many health care organizations are simply lost, using past approaches, which to their horror, no longer work in the new reality.

GOAL-ACHIEVING BLUEPRINT   141

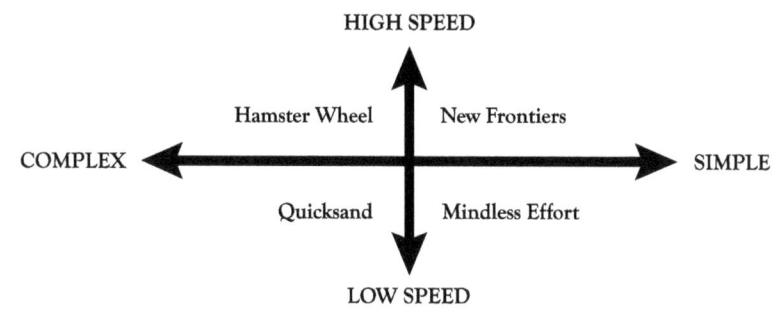

```
                      HIGH SPEED
                          ▲
        Hamster Wheel  |  New Frontiers
COMPLEX ◄─────────────┼──────────────► SIMPLE
          Quicksand    |  Mindless Effort
                          ▼
                      LOW SPEED
```

Figure 10.1 Impact of speed and simplicity on strategy execution power

With plentiful speed but lacking simplicity, you may find yourself running frantically in a hamster wheel. The abundance of organizational activity doesn't bring you closer to achieving your most important goals. Complicated effort is rewarded over simple results. For example, you saw earlier that more than $130 billion is spent yearly on more and more sophisticated training all over the world, with very little return on investment.

A simple yet slow operation leads to mindless effort. Activities are well-defined, but sense of urgency is lacking. Many government bureaucracies typically operate in this environment. These organizations have fallen in love with the quality of their processes, instead of falling in love with their clients.

Finally, when speed and simplicity come together, you're operating on new frontiers where great things may happen. Strategy is clearly defined, growth goals are preeminent, and execution is effortless and effective.

How to Build an Execution Engine

Regardless of where you find yourself and your organization on your strategy execution power, there is always opportunity to improve. What if you could build an execution engine based on simplicity and speed, which almost automatically ensures that only the most important things get done in an organization? This approach is what I call *selective strategy execution*.

The first important element for selective strategy execution is focus. Peter Drucker, the eminent management thinker, once observed that senior executives should focus on only one strategic goal. You can't ride two bikes at the same time. You came across this one thing in Chapter 2: the

Major Definite Purpose. Usually all other strategic objectives support this one objective.

Executive Question

Which one growth goal, that if achieved right here, right now, would have the biggest positive impact on your organization?

The second critical element of selective strategy execution is behavior. You will never get the new results you want from the existing behaviors that you like. In other words, culture (the mindsets governing behaviors) eats strategy for breakfast. A new strategic goal always requires building a new set of behaviors. These behaviors need to be role-modeled by every senior executive. After all, the minimum effective behavior you show yourself is the maximum effective behavior you can expect from others.

Executive Question

Which one behavior would have the biggest positive impact on achieving your most important strategic goal?

The third essential element of selective strategy execution is rhythmic, compound improvement. Small improvements will have big impact over time due to the compound effect. As shown earlier, the UK rowing team was used to a lackluster performance in the Olympics. In 1998, the team made a decision to do things differently: as of that moment, every action would be judged against the question, "Will it make the boat go faster?" This created a rhythmic and relentless focus on small effectiveness improvements and was the recipe to Olympic Gold in 2000.

Executive Question

Which actions can you take daily to achieve your most important goal and build the most important behaviors for yourself or your organization within 100 days?

These three questions form the heart of an execution engine. Figure 10.2 illustrates the three building blocks of selective strategy execution.

> ONE GOAL ➤ ONE BEHAVIOR ➤ 100 DAYS ➤

Figure 10.2 The three building blocks of selective strategy execution

Case Study
How to Put Selective Strategy Execution in Action

A client of mine was running a highly successful service business, catering to global Fortune 2000 companies. However, the company had reached a revenue plateau, and wanted to change things quickly. It had an excellent product, a solid strategy, but were still stuck. Then I noticed two interesting things. First, the organization rapidly came together in times of crisis or urgent need. Second, its senior management quickly lost focus on the strategy, becoming overly eager when even remote new opportunities presented themselves. Would it be possible to use the strength of the company's collaborative spirit and, at the same time, eliminate the weakness of easy distraction, to create a constant sense of urgency to get things done and stay the course? The answer was selective strategy execution implemented with a few steps.

The first step was to focus on the most important strategic goal. So we asked the question: Which one growth goal that, if achieved right here, right now, would have the biggest positive impact on this organization? After some thought, the answer was actually quite simple: If the company could increase its number of long-term clients by 50 percent, it would break through their revenue ceiling. Thus, increasing the number of long-term Fortune 2000 clients became the major definite purpose (MDP).

The second step was to identify the behaviors necessary to make this strategic goal happen. Therefore, we asked the question: Which one behavior, if we show it consistently in our organization, will have the biggest positive impact? To make the most out of this question, we needed to make use of behavioral distinctions. As discussed earlier, a behavioral distinction draws a clear border between good behavior and the best behavior. The most important behavioral distinction for this company was the difference between pleasing and serving a prospect. Pleasing means giving what the prospect *wants*. Serving is much more valuable, because you provide what the prospect *needs*. In this case, a practical application of serving behavior was to consistently refuse giving proposals and quotes to gatekeepers (people who can say no, but can't say yes), but always talk to the actual decision makers (people invested in the results of their services). This step required courage: As you can imagine, with this selective client approach, the biggest fear was losing actual, easy business.

Finally, we addressed the question "Will it make the boat go faster" with a 100-day challenge, called *Start Fast, Finish Strong*. In this challenge, we created a recurring strategic review and focused all leadership actions on one question: "Will this help achieve our major definite purpose and build successful behaviors?"

The results were remarkable. Within three months, 50 percent more long-term clients were added to the list. Not only that, but by focusing on behaviors around serving, both price and margins of existing client engagements increased significantly. Finally, a lot of frustration and work were saved by no longer putting time and energy in submitting proposals to lousy prospects.

How to Extend the Blueprint for Selective Strategy Execution

The executive questions to building an execution engine provide the framework to achieve your biggest growth goal. It's time to extend this framework further and make it more granular. First, by filling in details regarding the building blocks of goal-achieving: clarity, focus, and execution. Second, by applying the strengths of business leaders with engineering backgrounds: reality-based thinking, process design, and accelerated learning.

Clarity

To get clarity as a leader, you will have to define your most important goal, your major definite purpose. Key questions to define the most important goal:

- Which one growth goal would have the biggest positive impact on my business?

- If I could change one thing to dramatically improve my business, what would it be?
- What would I set out to achieve if I knew I couldn't fail?
- How would this goal apply to my strengths and the strengths of my organization?

The next step is to apply reality-based thinking. Key questions are:

- Has it been done before? If so, what is the baseline to achieve the goal?
- How will you know when you have achieved the goal?
- What exactly would be the difference between the old situation and the new situation?

After getting clarity on the goal, it's now time to get clarity on the behaviors that support the goal. The key question is:

- Which one organizational behavior, If I could change right here, right now, would help most to achieve the major definite purpose?

Focus

In preparing to cross the Valley of Death, your first approach is to use your process design strength to develop options:

- How can we apply triage to minimize the risks and maximize the gains before crossing the Valley of Death?
- How can we build a portfolio of options to achieve the goal?

Then decide how to allocate resources, diversify with portfolio thinking, and minimize energy:

- How would we allocate our time, energy, and money between risky new goals and existing operations?
- What are the vital few initiatives in our portfolio that will give us the majority of results?

The next step is to build language and metaphors by applying distinctions:

- What would the new culture that accompanies this big goal look like?
- Which behavioral distinctions would help us most to consistently show the most important new behavior?

Finally, apply strategic quitting to let go in order to reach out:

- What are the milestone criteria to kill any alternatives to achieve this goal?
- What can we delegate, eliminate, or outsource to free up time, energy, and money?

Execution

Now it's time to get going. These questions will prepare for obstacles and help overcome setbacks. Here's where you can use accelerated learning:

- What are our blind spots resulting from a pre-mortem exercise?
- Which one organizational Kryptonite habit needs to be eliminated to make the new goal happen?
- Which one personal Kryptonite habit must be eliminated to make the new goal happen?
- Which parts of the referral engine will help me most to quickly get new customers and grow the business?

The final questions to make selective strategy execution happen are:

- Which part of the one growth goal will help my organization most and can be achieved within 100 days?
- Which one behavior do I need to drive as a leader to make this goal happen?
- How can I use a spider line and set up a system of rhythmic compound improvement to reach the 100-day objective?

Why Selective Strategy Execution Builds on Engineering Strengths

Selective strategy execution is a powerful tool for business leaders to quickly make huge progress in complex organizations toward their most important strategic goals. On paper, it's deceptively easy, yet implementation walks a fine line between failure and success. You should make your strategy as simple as possible and go as fast as you can.

The selective strategy execution approach really makes a difference for leaders with an engineering background for a few reasons.

First, the natural impulse for any organization is to add complexity to manage complex systems. This is actually counter-effective. Did the introduction of the new and vastly better Human Resources IT package really improve actual adherence to individual personal development plans? Probably not. Instead, simplicity is a very refreshing approach to get things done. If you have only one objective, decision making becomes easy. Instead of gradually moving a wide range of strategic initiatives, use the reality principle to apply the incredible power of the spear tip: massive action centered on the most important goal.

Next, selective strategy execution applies process design, because it's focused on systematically building new behaviors in the entire organization. This reason is often the missing part of any strategy. When was the last time you saw a strategic plan where the biggest amount of time and effort was dedicated to building new behaviors? As apparent from the case study, these behaviors are not only essential to achieve your big goals, but often have a wide-ranging positive impact on other parts of the organization as well.

Finally, building new behaviors is the cornerstone for rhythmic, compound improvement. It keeps strategy top-of-mind, not only for senior executives, but also for every employee. By focusing on role modeling the desired behaviors every single day, a senior executive is therefore able to change the entire organization in a positive way. Role-modeling is how you put your strengths of accelerated learning into practice.

How to Expand Your Impact as a Business Leader

This book started with a question: How can business leaders with an engineering past apply their strengths to accelerate their career trajectories?

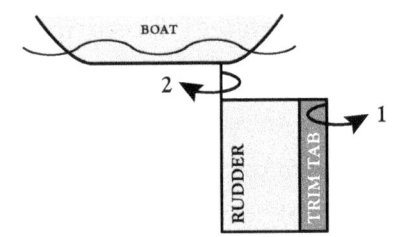

Figure 10.3 Trim tab in a rudder of a boat

You've seen that there is a method to the madness. My objective was to organize the nonobvious and make this method transparent. Doing so required a different framework: the combination of the three building blocks of goal achieving—clarity, focus, and execution—with the three strengths of leaders with engineering backgrounds—reality-based thinking, process design, and accelerated learning. These six elements drive great business leadership and help you to become an unstoppable goal achiever.

Yet, once you start working with these six elements and adopt this way of thinking to grow your business and grow as a leader, something else will happen as well: You will massively influence your organization. The reason is that the minimum effective behavior you adopt yourself is the maximum effective behavior you can expect from others. This is good news. By changing your minimum standards, you'll suddenly be able to change the entire organization. This effect is called *trim tab leadership*. The principle of a trim tab is illustrated in Figure 10.3.

A trim tab is a small rudder placed on a big rudder of a large ship. By changing the direction of the trim tab (1) you change the direction of the big rudder and (2) which changes the course of a large ship. Your conscious decision to act as a trim tab and improve yourself as a leader will have a huge impact on your entire environment. This practice is how successful engineers expand their impact and become great business leaders.

Summary of How Engineers Become Business Leaders

Here are the 10 principles that describe how successful engineers become great business leaders:

1. Business leadership success is determined by talent, luck, and skill. Choose an area that is a natural fit for your talents, where the impact of luck is minimized, and skills can be quickly expanded.
2. You don't need to become twice as good to double your results. Use the power laws of location, time, and knowledge to become slightly better in the few things that really matter to massively improve achievement.
3. Successful engineers are skilled at solving problems. Great business leaders with engineering backgrounds apply these skills to make the boat go faster. They use growth thinking and business development goals as the core of everything they do.
4. The higher the risk, the higher the reward. Divert part of your time and energy as a business leader from your current job, to more risky activities in the field of business development. At the same time, look for ways to reduce the downside of these activities.
5. The three building blocks of goal achieving are clarity, focus, and execution.
6. About clarity:
    a. You will not see how to do it until you see yourself doing it. Be clear on what achieving ambitious growth goals should look like.
    b. Use a spider line to measure progress on your goals.
7. About focus:
    a. The three universal strengths for engineers are reality-based thinking, process design, and accelerated learning. Focus on expanding these strengths and eliminating adverse behaviors that mask strengths.

b. Work on your business. Use your engineering strengths to support and drive three business growth activities: marketing, innovation, and strategy.
   c. The bigger the goal, the bigger the obstacles. This truth is called the Valley of Death. Use your engineering strengths to apply triage before committing to a big growth goal. Apply portfolio thinking to overcome obstacles on your way to achieve big goals.
8. About execution:
   a. You will never get the new results you want from the existing behaviors you like. Use your engineering strengths to create behavioral distinctions. Distinctions build the language, stories, and metaphors to role model the required leadership behaviors for yourself and your organization to achieve big goals.
   b. Doing more is no longer the answer to too much to do. Use your engineering strengths to apply strategic quitting. This action ensures that you maintain momentum by freeing up time, energy, and money to cross the Valley of Death.
   c. Be aware of your thinking biases and use your engineering strengths to notice when your intuitive operator, System One, goes off the rails and your lazy executive, System Two, needs to be activated to improve your judgment.
   d. Be aware of adverse leadership behaviors, which are caused by applying your strengths as engineers under the wrong circumstances.
   e. If you don't have a process for getting referrals, you are at the mercy of the processes of others for giving referrals. Use your engineering strengths to build a referral engine to get new customers quickly and bring in business easily to support your growth goals.
9. Adopt a spear tip, not a tidal wave. Use your engineering strengths to design a selective strategy execution blueprint and become an unstoppable goal achiever. Get your most important strategic goals done in the shortest amount of time with the least amount of energy.
10. Be a trim tab to change an entire organization. The minimum effective behaviors you demonstrate as a business leader are the maximum effective behaviors you can expect from other people.

30 Executive Questions to Improve Your Business Leadership

1. What are your prime chunks of time as a business leader and how can you maximize their effect?
2. Which additional knowledge would have an exponential impact on your achievement as a business leader?
3. What spider line do you need as a leader to monitor progress on your most important goals and spring into action as soon as a deviation occurs?
4. What should not work, but is working anyway? How can you apply reverse engineering to systematically obtain more of these excellent results?
5. How can you design and apply quick pilots with fast, sizeable, and frequent feedback, to accelerate learning for you and your organization?
6. Where do you reward behaviors in your organization, focused on playing to win, acting boldly, and courageously moving ahead into the unknown?
7. What is the biggest issue your business is facing right now? How can you apply your three engineering strengths to act more like an owner and less like a victim to deal with this issue?
8. Where do you need to force yourself and your organization to behave like a student, instead of a follower? Where do you need to step out of dogmatic thinking and become more curious instead?
9. Where do you need to raise the bar as a leader to stop symbolism and start to provide substance by consciously role-modeling the behaviors you would like to see on a consistent basis?
10. Is your entire organization committed to, or only involved in its most important goal? Which behavior can you show as a leader to increase commitment?

11. In what areas of your business are you pleasing when you should instead be serving?
12. Where has your organization fallen in love with processes and lost sight of the overall result?
13. Where can you improve your key presentations, take less space, and focus more on adding value to your customers?
14. What behaviors bring out the best in your team members, and how can you speak with clarity to make these behaviors explicit?
15. If agreements are ignored often in your organization, which standards do you set for honoring your word as a leader?
16. When should you be more curious, rely less on anecdotes and ask, "Where's the evidence for that?"
17. Which legacy do you want to leave behind as a business leader?
18. How would you apply strategic quitting regarding the performance review system to improve the speed and quality of feedback in your organization?
19. Where can you use 20 percent of the effort to quickly meet 80 percent of the cost-saving objectives?
20. Where can you use your engineering strengths to delegate, eliminate, and outsource to free up time for yourself and focus on marketing, innovation, and strategy?
21. To avoid being blinded by coherent stories, improve executive judgment, and find missing parts of a corporate strategy, you need to ask:
    a. What else can explain these data points? This question uncovers lack of alternative explanations for stated facts.
    b. What needs to happen to ruin this strategy? This information points to vague or missing assumptions.
    c. Who has tried before and has failed? This knowledge will prevent you from ignoring historic trends and developments.
    d. Why are you using impossibly accurate numbers (like market share will grow to 24.89 percent in 5 years, really?). This question challenges mindless extrapolation of uncertain data.
22. What needs to happen to abandon your most important initiative? How do you check this progress on a regular basis?
23. Where do you gild the lily and allow your organization to continue tinkering with what actually works well?

24. In your next interaction, when should you skip the sledge hammer and apply tact and empathy to bring your message across?
25. How do you know you have crossed the line between admirable persistence and block-headed tenacity?
26. Where are you trying to win, when this area is actually irrelevant for your success as a business leader?
27. Where do you try to look smart instead of being effective as a business leader?
28. Which one growth goal, that if achieved right here, right now, would have the biggest positive impact on your organization?
29. Which one behavior would have the biggest positive impact on achieving your most important strategic goal?
30. Which massive actions can you take daily to achieve your most important goal and build the most important behaviors for yourself or your organization within 100 days?

Summary of the Goal-Achieving Blueprint

Building block	Key question
Clarity	Which one growth goal would have the biggest positive impact on my business?
	If I could change one thing to dramatically improve my business, what would it be?
	What would I set out to achieve if I knew I couldn't fail?
	How would this goal apply to my strengths and the strengths of my organization?
	Has it been done before? If so, what is the baseline to achieve the goal?
	How will you know when you have achieved the goal?
	What would be the difference between the old situation and the new situation?
	Which one organizational behavior, If I could change right here, right now, would help most to achieve the major definite purpose?
Focus	How can we apply triage to minimize the risks and maximize the gains while crossing the Valley of Death?
	How can we build a portfolio of options to achieve the goal?
	How would we allocate our time, energy, and money between risky new goals and existing operations?
	What are the vital few initiatives in our portfolio that will give us the majority of results?
	What would the new culture that accompanies this big goal look like?
	Which behavioral distinctions would help us most to consistently show the most important new behavior?
	What are the milestone criteria to kill any alternatives to achieve this goal?
	What can we delegate, eliminate, or outsource to free up time, energy, and money?

(continued)

Building block	Key question
Execution	What are our blind spots resulting from a pre-mortem exercise?
	Which one organizational Kryptonite habit needs to be eliminated to make the new goal happen?
	Which one personal Kryptonite habit must be eliminated to make the new goal happen?
	Which parts of the referral engine will help me most to quickly get new customers and grow the business?
	Which part of the one growth goal will help my organization most and can be achieved within 100 days?
	Which one behavior do I need to drive as a leader to make this goal happen?
	How can I set up a spider line and a system of rhythmic compound improvement to reach the 100-day objective?

Recommended Reading

Bernstein, W. 2010. *The Four Pillars of Investing*. New York: McGraw-Hill Education.
Cialdini, R.B. 2007. *Influence*. New York: HarperCollins Publishers.
Djukich, D. 2011. *Straight-Line Leadership*. Bandon: Robert D. Reed Publishers.
Godin, S. 2007. *The Dip*. London: Piatkus Books.
Goldsmith, M. 2007. *What Got You Here Won't Get You There*. New York: Hyperion.
Kahneman, D. 2011. *Thinking, Fast and Slow*. New York: Penguin Publishing.
Koch, R. 2000. *The Power Laws*. London: Nicholas Brealey Publishing.
Medina, J. 2008. *Brain Rules*. Seattle: Pear Press.
Rulkens, P. 2017. *The Power of Preeminence*. Deventer: Vakmedianet.
Taleb, N. 2010. *The Black Swan*. New York: Random House Trade Paperbacks.
Tracy, B. 2004. *Goals!* San Francisco: Berrett-Koehler Publishers.
Weiss, A. 2003. *Million Dollar Consulting*. New York: McGraw-Hill.

About the Author

How do the best get better? Companies like KPMG, ExxonMobil, and Novartis continue to work with **Paul Rulkens** to raise the bar and quickly bring results to the next level.

Paul knows that doing more is no longer the default answer to too much to do. He is an expert in high performance: the art and science of accelerating bold executive outcomes with the least amount of effort. He is an award-winning professional speaker, international author, and a trusted boardroom advisor who has helped thousands of business executives, managers, and professionals get everything they can out of everything they have. His ideas to improve results and accelerate careers are often described as thought-provoking and counterintuitive, yet highly effective.

You do not have to be sick in order to get better. As an international keynote speaker, Paul annually addresses dozens of successful international audiences about essential mindsets and proven strategies to reap exponential business improvements. His most popular topics cover the secrets of consistent execution, easy innovation, powerful leadership, business growth, career acceleration, and seamless teamwork.

Originally trained as a chemical engineer, Paul's work is based on deep knowledge and extensive experience in the practical business applications of behavioral psychology, neuroscience and, especially, common sense. His popular TED talks are used frequently in professional training sessions all over the world.

He is the cofounder of Quantum Leap: a master program to accelerate the careers of high-potential leaders with an engineering background.

His clients call his keynotes both substantive and hilarious. The reason may be that Paul once was trained as a standup comedian, receiving critical acclaim for his Arnold Schwarzenegger impersonation. However, the miserable failure of his ensuing pumping iron muscle development project prevented him from pursuing his true calling in life: a career as a credible Arnold Schwarzenegger body double . . . .

More information about Paul and his work can be found on www.paulrulkens.com

Index

Accelerated learning, 42–44
　applying, 44–46
　business application, 46
　feedback and, 43–44
　leadership skills, and behaviors, 46
　and myopic thinking, 109–111
　and planning fallacy, 108–109
Achievement, 4–5
　approaches for maximizing, 10–11
　law of risk and reward for, 9–10
Actions, 21
Active listening, 33
Activity, versus goal, 56
Add value, versus taking up space, 79
Adverse habits
　butterflies in wrong stomach, 116–117
　excessive Ahabism, 121–122
　foie gras persuasion, 117–118
　gilding lily, 119–120
　landing without skill, 120–121
　lost in logic, 118
　Mensa madness, 124
　overview of, 115–116
　perfection before production, 118–119
　solution monopolist, 123
　winners addiction, 122–123
All-round leadership excellence, is myth, 35–36
AlphaGo, 42–43
Anecdotes, versus evidence, 81
Artificial intelligence (AI), 42–43
Asset allocation, 58
Assumptions, and reality-based thinking, 37
Authority, 129, 131–132

Banner, work under different, 54
Baseless exuberance, 105–106

Baseline thinking, for planning fallacy, 56, 109
Behavior
　importance of, 28–29
　and selective strategy execution, 142
Behavioral distinction, 73
　on organizational culture, impact of, 82
Beliefs, 28
Berkhout, Marcel, interview of, 66–67
Bhakta, Paresh, interview of, 134–135
Biases, defined, 102
Big business goals
　achievement, 4–5
　extraordinary achievements, small differences create, 9
　introduction to, 3–4
　law of risk and reward for, 9–10
　maximizing results, approaches for, 10–11
　power laws for, 7–8
　right goals, selection of, 11–14
　skill and talent, overestimation of, 6–7
Boost signal, and effective leadership behavior, 69–70
Breedveld, Stépan, interview of, 113–114
Building legacy, versus leaving trail, 82–83
Business leader
　expanding your impact as, 147–148
　important task of, 41
Business process review (BPR), 34
Business stakeholders, 127
Butterflies in wrong stomach, 116–117

Campfire songs organization, 20
Cargo cult thinking, 6–7, 103
Chalk outline, 27

162 INDEX

Clarity, and goal-achieving, 144–145, 155
Client connections
  authority, 129, 131–132
  building trust, 128–129
  consistency, 129, 130
  liking, 129, 131
  overview of, 127–128
  reciprocation, 129
  referrals, 128
  scarcity, 129, 132–133
  social proof, 129, 130–131
Cognitive bias, 6
Cognitive dissonance, 104–106
Columbus confusion, 72
Committed, versus involved, 77–78
Compound improvement, and selective strategy execution, 142
Confession parameter, 27
Connection, 19–20
Consistency, 129, 130
Corporate fantasy, and Valley of Death, 55
Cost reduction, 58–59, 94
Culture, elements of, 73
Customers, and strategic quitting, 93–94

Decision boldness. See Triage
Decisions driven by data, 37
Delayed learning, 43–44
Delegation, 96–97
Digital problems, 61
Direct measurement, for goals, 27
Diversification, 58
Do-or-die strategy. See Strategic boldness
Doomsday beliefs, 104–106
Doomsday thinking, 105
Dunning–Kruger effect, 6

Effective training, 92
Effectiveness, and executive judgment, 38–40
80/20 rule, 7, 91–92
Elimination, and strategic quitting, 97
Emotional quotient (EQ), 33–34
Engineered process, 42

Engineering strengths
  accelerated learning, 42–46
  all-round leadership excellence, is myth, 35–36
  deploying your, 47–48
  developing strengths, 33–34
  driving growth goals, 48–50
  process design, 40–42
  reality-based thinking, 37–40
  recognizing super-talents, 36
Evidence versus anecdotes, 81
Excessive Ahabism, 121–122
Execution, and goal-achieving, 146, 156
Executive judgment, 38
  accelerated learning, overcomes myopic thinking, 109–111
  planning fallacy, 108–109
  faculty, engaging your, 101–103
  implementing process, to avoid mistakes, 111–112
  overview of, 101
  process design, overcomes mental substitution, 107–108
  reality-based thinking, overcomes cognitive dissonance, 104–106
  coherent stories, fallacy of, 103–104
  Semmelweis reflex, 106–107
Exploring options, 61
External measurement, for goals, 27
Extraordinary achievements, small differences and, 9

Failing fast, 64
Failure, common-cause, 64
Feasibility, and executive judgment, 38–40
Feedback, and accelerated learning, 43–44
Feelings, 21
Flash testing, 44, 46
Focus, and selective strategy execution, 141–142, 145–146, 155
Foie gras, 117–118
Follower, versus student, 75–76
Fuzzy problems, 61

Giving your word, versus honoring your word, 80–81
Go, board game, 42–43
Goal
  versus activity, 56
  measuring progress on, 26–28
Goal-achieving blueprint
  building blocks of, 144–146, 155–156
  business leader, expanding your impact as, 147–148
  overview of, 139–140
  selective strategy execution. See Selective strategy execution
  speed, and simplicity, importance of, 140–141
Go/no go criteria, 117
Good plan, 63
Good vision, 22
Growth goals, 48–50
  applying strategic quitting for, 89–91

Hallway lip service, 53
Hedgehog reflex, 54
High-performance organization, 50
High-performance team, 24
Honoring your word, versus giving your word, 80–81
Human brain, simplified model of, 56–57

Imminent failure, warning signs of, 53–54
Inclusive teamwork, 33
Indirect measurement, for goals, 27
Information graveyard, 54
Innovation, 48, 93
Intermediate predefined milestone, 63
Internal measurement, for goals, 27
Involved, versus committed, 77–78

Jian, interview of, 83–84

Kregting, Aloys, interview of, 98–99
Kryptonite habits, 115–116, 125
  butterflies in wrong stomach, 116–117
  excessive Ahabism, 121–122
  foie gras persuasion, 117–118
  gilding lily, 119–120
  landing without skill, 120–121
  lost in logic, 118
  Mensa madness, 124
  perfection before production, 118–119
  solution monopolist, 123
  winners addiction, 122–123

Law of risk and reward, 9–10
Leadership behaviors, effective
  add value versus taking up space, 79
  boost signal and, 69–70
  building a legacy versus leaving a trail, 82–83
  committed versus involved, 77–78
  decreasing noise, 70–71
  evidence versus anecdotes, 81
  honouring your word versus giving your word, 80–81
  overview of, 69
  ownership versus victimhood, 75
  playing to win versus playing not to lose, 73–74
  poka yoke, principles of, 71–72
  results versus process, 78–79
  serving versus pleasing, 78
  speaking with clarity versus speaking in code, 80
  student versus follower, 75–76
  substance versus symbolism, 76–77
Leadership, twin engines of, 19–20
Leaving a trail, versus building a legacy, 82–83
Liking, 129, 131
Lily gilding, 119–120
Lizard brain, 56–57, 88
Logic, lost in, 118
Luck, for achievement, 4–5

Magical thinking, 38–39
Marketing, 48
Meetings, purpose of, 95
Mensa madness, 124
Mental substitution, 107–108

Mindsets, 28
  to achieve goals, importance
    of, 21–22
Momentum fallacy, 90
Moral licensing, 76
Myopic optimization, 62

Natural laws, 45
Neocortex, 56
Noise, and effective leadership
    behavior, 70–71
Norms, 110

Obsession, 36
Oostwegel, Erik, interview of,
    125–126
Options, defined, 59
Organizational culture
  behavioral distinctions, impact of, 82
  Kryptonite habits, impact of, 125
Organizational goals, clarity
    on, 25–26
Organizational paralysis, 57
Outsourcing, 97
Overcoming obstacles
  achieving goals, options for, 59–61
  decisions for, 64–65
  new initiatives, failure of, 56–57
  reasons for, 53–55
  Valley of Death. See Valley of Death
Ownership, versus victimhood, 75

Pareto rule, 7
Pattern recognition, for problem
    solving, 45–46
Peak performance fallacy, 34
Perfect clarity
  on behaviors, 28–29
  on measuring growth progress,
    26–28
  mindsets to achieve goals, 21–22
  on organizational goals, 25–26
  overview of, 19–20
  on personal goals, 23–24
  on team goals, 24–25
  on vision, 22–23
Performance review, 92–93
Personal goals, clarity on, 23–24

Planning fallacy, 55–56
  accelerated learning and, 108–109
  baseline thinking for, 56
Plausibility, 108–109
Playing not to lose, versus playing to
    win, 73–74
Playing to win, versus playing not to
    lose, 73–74
Pleasing, versus serving, 78
Poka yoke, principles of, 71–72
Portfolio thinking, 47, 61, 63
Power law
  of prime knowledge, 8
  of prime location, 7–8
  of prime time, 8
Pre-mortem exercise, 111–112
Probability, 108–109
Process
  defined, 40
  design, engineering strength, 40–41
  applying, 42
  business application, 46
  leadership skills, and behaviors, 46
  versus results, 78–79
Procrastination, 56, 88
  strategies to overcome, 58–59
Production, perfection before,
    118–119
Psychology of achievement, 21

Quick goal exercise, 23–24

Razor's edge, 9
Reality-based thinking, 45
  applying, 38–40
  business application, 46
  and cognitive dissonance,
    104–106
  and coherent stories, fallacy
    of, 103–104
  components of, 37–38
  leadership skills, and behaviors, 46
  and Semmelweis reflex, 106–107
Reciprocation, 129
Referral, 128
Reporting, and strategic quitting,
    95–96
Restart button, 54

Results, 21
  versus process, 78–79
Reverse countdown, 53
Reverse engineered process, 42
Right goals, selection of, 11–14
Risk, downside, ways to mitigate, 13
Role model, 29
Rosetto, Luca, interview of, 51–52
Rules of thumb, 45–46

Safe endeavor, 47–48
Sanders, Jan-Willem, x
Scarcity, 129, 132–133
Scientism, 103–104
Selective strategy execution, 141
  case study for, 143–144
  elements for, 141–143
  and engineering strengths, 147
  extending blueprint for, 144–146
Self-selecting bias, 37–38
Semmelweis reflex, 106–107
Servant leadership, 33
Serving, versus pleasing, 78
Shallow learning, 43
Simplicity, 71–72, 140–141
Skill
  for achievement, 4–5
  landing without, 120–121
  overestimation of, 6–7
Slow learning, 43
Smoking gun, 27
Social proof, 129, 130–131
Soft skills, 33–34
Solution monopolist, 123
Speaking in code versus with clarity, 80
Speed, 140–141
Spider line, for leader, 28
Standardization, poka yoke element, 72
Stock market, long-term investing in, 47
Strategic boldness, 62
Strategic quitting
  for achieving strategic goals, 89–91
  effectiveness of, 88–89
  in job, applying, 96–97
  in organization, applying, 91–96
  overview of, 87–88

Strategy, 48
Strategy execution, 139–140
Student, versus follower, 75–76
Substance, versus symbolism, 76–77
Success, common-cause, 64
Super-talents, 36
Superman stereotype, 34
Symbolic thinking, 39
Symbolism, versus substance, 76–77
Systematic behavior testing, 41
Systematic thinking bias, 37–38

Taking up space, versus add
  value, 79
Talent, for achievement, 4–5
  overestimation of, 6–7
Team goals, clarity on, 24–25
Thinking filters, 22
Thoughts, and achievement, 21
Time horizons, 64
Trim tab leadership, 148
Trust building, 128–129
  elements of, 129–133

Utopian thinking, 39

Valley of Death, 54–55
  applying alternatives while crossing, 63–64
  corporate fantasy and, 55
  exploring options before entering into, 61–62
  ignoring, is dangerous, 55–56
  strategic quitting and, 87–97
  strategies to overcome, 58–59
Victimhood, versus ownership, 75
Vision, 19–20
  creating a, 22–23
Vital few phenomenon, 7, 64
Volvo, 44

Winners addiction, 122–123
Working in versus on business, 48–49

Zero-based thinking, 90–91

OTHER TITLES IN THE HUMAN RESOURCE MANAGEMENT AND ORGANIZATIONAL BEHAVIOR COLLECTION

- *The Concise Coaching Handbook: How to Coach Yourself and Others to Get Business Results* by Elizabeth Dickinson
- *Lead Self First Before Leading Others: A Life Planning Resource* by Stephen K. Hacker
- *The How of Leadership: Inspire People to Achieve Extraordinary Results* by Maxwell Ubah
- *Managing Organizational Change: The Measurable Benefits of Applied iOCM* by Linda C. Mattingly
- *Creating the Accountability Culture: The Science of Life Changing Leadership* by Yvonnne Thompson
- *Conflict and Leadership: How to Harness the Power of Conflict to Create Better Leaders and Build Thriving Teams* by Christian Muntean
- *Precision Recruitment Skills: How to Find the Right Person For the Right Job, the First Time* by Rod Matthews
- *Practical Performance Improvement: How to Be an Exceptional People Manager* by Rod Matthews
- *Creating Leadership: How to Change Hippos Into Gazelles* by Philip Goodwin and Tony Page
- *Uncovering the Psychology of Good Bosses vs Bad Bosses and What it Means for Leaders: How to Avoid the High Cost of Bad Leadership* by Debra Dupree
- *Competency Based Education: How to Prepare College Graduates for the World of Work* by Nina Morel and Bruce Griffiths
- *Phenomenology and Its Application in Business* by Roger Sages and Abhishek Goel
- *Organizational Design in Business: A New Alternative for a Complex World* by Carrie Foster
- *The 360 Degree CEO: Generating Profits While Leading and Living with Passion and Principles* by Lorraine A. Moore

Announcing the Business Expert Press Digital Library

Concise e-books business students need for classroom and research

This book can also be purchased in an e-book collection by your library as

- a one-time purchase,
- that is owned forever,
- allows for simultaneous readers,
- has no restrictions on printing, and
- can be downloaded as PDFs from within the library community.

Our digital library collections are a great solution to beat the rising cost of textbooks. E-books can be loaded into their course management systems or onto students' e-book readers. The **Business Expert Press** digital libraries are very affordable, with no obligation to buy in future years. For more information, please visit www.businessexpertpress.com/librarians. To set up a trial in the United States, please email sales@businessexpertpress.com.

Lightning Source UK Ltd.
Milton Keynes UK
UKHW020610310719
347141UK00005B/253/P